THE BATTLE OF BRITAIN YEARBOOK

THE BATTLE OF BRITAIN YEARBOOK

PETER R. MARCH

Cover illustrations: *Front*: Spitfire over London. (© Wilfred Harevy, GAvA); *rear*: No 85 Sqn Hurricane pilots scramble at Martlesham Heath.

First published 2015

The History Press
The Mill, Brimscombe Port
Stroud, Gloucestershire, GL5 2QG
www.thehistorypress.co.uk

British Library Cataloguing in Publication Data.
A catalogue record for this book is available from the British Library.

ISBN 978 0 7509 6390 9

Typesetting and origination by The History Press
Printed and bound in Malta, by Melita Press

CONTENTS

Supermarine Spitfires had a pivotal role in the Battle of Britain.

ACKNOWLEDGEMENTS

I am indebted to Paul Fiddian and Brian Strickland for the considerable help I have received from them with the research, collation and checking of detailed facts in the preparation of this book. I gratefully acknowledge the assistance of Michael J.F. Bowyer in the compilation of the Battle of Britain timeline and the portrait of Duxford at war first published in the *Royal Air Force Yearbook*. I would also like to thank Daniel March and David Donald for providing details of the Luftwaffe's organisation, aircraft, and facts and figures. The Royal Air Force Museum, London, and the Imperial War Museum, Duxford, have provided an invaluable resource.

The difficult task of sourcing and selecting photographs has been greatly helped by Michael Bowyer, Denis Calvert, Tom Cole, Jarrod Cotter, Graham Finch, Jonathan Falconer, Paul Fiddian, Andrew March, Daniel March, Leo Marriott, Col Pope, Brian Strickland and Richard L. Ward, who have supplied many of the illustrations from their respective personal collections. The front cover artwork is from a series of original paintings by Wilfred Hardy, GAvA, produced in 2000 for the publication *Fight of the Few*.

Peter R. March

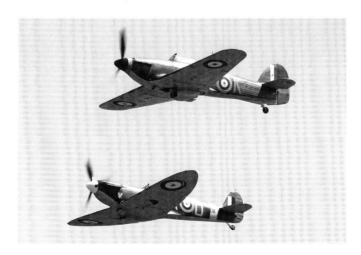

A battle-winning partnership: Hawker Hurricane and Supermarine Spitfire.

INTRODUCTION

H aving investigated and written about the Battle of Britain over many years, I am pleased to present an up-to-date look at some of the key factors that enabled the RAF to stop the Luftwaffe from gaining air superiority and in so doing prevent Hitler's army from crossing the English Channel and invading Great Britain. Without the bravery of the RAF's 'few' young pilots, the skill of its leaders, and the application of new technologies such as radar, innovative communications, command and control, this success would not have been achieved. Neither would it have been possible if we had remained stuck in the biplane era. Without the talents of Sydney Camm, Reginald Mitchell and their colleagues at Hawker and Supermarine, together with Sir Henry Royce's brilliant team at Rolls-Royce who developed the Merlin engine, we would not have had the Hurricane and Spitfire, which were able to take on the incoming formations of German bombers and dogfight with their escorting Messerschmitt fighters.

Gladiator, Spitfire and Hurricane. The bold step from biplane to monoplane fighter was decisive.

As you look at the Battle of Britain some seventy-five years after it ended, you discover many new facts, but you also uncover a lot of conflicting accounts of the same actions from the RAF and Luftwaffe; not least of these are the discrepancies between pilots' claims about the numbers of aircraft shot down compared with the actual losses in official post-war records. In many cases the daily claims in the battle were some three or four times higher than the actual figures in the Luftwaffe's records. No one should make any false assumptions about these discrepancies. Both sides in the conflict presented numbers that their leaders wanted the general public to believe. What was really important in the end was how effective, or not, the opposing air forces had been in achieving their objectives on each day.

The Battle of Britain, fought between July and October 1940, was one of the decisive events of the Second World War. Not only was it the first battle ever to have been fought almost exclusively in the air, it ultimately stopped Hitler's plans to invade and subjugate Great Britain as he already had Poland, Czechoslovakia, Belgium, Holland, Denmark, Norway and France.

Hermann Göring told Hitler that the Luftwaffe could destroy the RAF in a matter of weeks. He was soon proved wrong as the seemingly endless waves of attacking Junkers, Dornier and Heinkel

Queen Elizabeth, King George VI and Lord Dowding.

bombers, with their Messerschmitt fighter escorts, were met by squadrons of Hurricanes and Spitfires. Heavily outnumbered, the success of these young pilots in the aerial battle was significantly enhanced by the RAF's command and control system using radar and effective radio communications. Exhausted pilots flew one mission after another, pausing only long enough for their aircraft to be refuelled. Some were shot down but after parachuting to safety were quickly back in the air again.

The Battle of Britain came to its climax in September 1940 as the RAF reached a crisis point. Mercifully, the Luftwaffe failed to 'close down' the RAF, despite coming close, in part because Hitler became impatient and switched the bombers away to the blitz on towns and cities. Failing to have mastery of the air over southern England and the Channel prevented the invasion of Britain. On 17 September, Hitler ordered that the planned invasion of Britain (Operation *Sea Lion*), that had been poised across the Channel for three months, be postponed until further notice – the tide had turned and the Battle of Britain won, but at a very high cost to aircrew from both air arms. Of the 3,080 Allied aircrew from fourteen countries who flew in the four months of the battle, 537 lost their lives and many more were seriously injured. The RAF lost 902, mostly single-seat, fighters, while the Luftwaffe lost 1,598 aircraft – many of which were multi-crew bombers.

The whole fury and might of the enemy must very soon be turned on us.

Hitler knows that he will have to break us in this island or lose the war. If we can stand up to him, all Europe may be free and the life of the world may move forward into broad, sunlit uplands. But if we fail, then the whole world, including the United States, including all that we have known and cared for, will sink into the abyss of a new Dark Age made more sinister, and perhaps more protracted, by the lights of perverted science.

Let us therefore brace ourselves to our duties, and so bear ourselves that, if the British Empire and its Commonwealth last for a thousand years, men will still say: 'This was their finest hour.'

Winston Churchill, 18 June 1940

Vapour trails over London left by dogfighting aircraft at the height of the battle.

1 PRELUDE

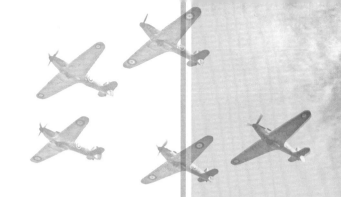

The Battle of Britain is of great significance not just in military terms but in terms of the United Kingdom as a whole. The air battle in the summer of 1940 was one of the decisive events of the Second World War. Upon its outcome depended the survival of Great Britain, with all the implications for the subsequent liberation of Western Europe and final victory by the Allies. It was the first battle ever to have been fought almost exclusively in the air, which makes it important in a historical sense, but its real significance was that it ultimately thwarted Hitler's plan to occupy and subjugate Great Britain.

Had it been solely a question of numbers, the RAF would have been in serious difficulties right from the start. In 1938, the RAF had believed it needed a minimum of fifty-two fighter squadrons for home defence against the Luftwaffe. By June 1940, it only had thirty-two, largely as a result of the campaign in France and the effort to protect the Dunkirk evacuation in particular. Of these squadrons, only twenty-five were made up of Hurricanes and Spitfires – less than half the strength that was really thought necessary.

The severe winter of 1939–40 was characterised by early and prolonged fog, frost and snow, which effectively restricted air operations over most of north-west Europe. It brought atrocious conditions to the ill-prepared airfields of France. The war began in earnest in April 1940 with the German attack on Denmark and Norway. Bomber Command made limited attacks on the German advance, but distance was a barrier. Some Gladiators and Hurricanes made heroic attempts to intervene, operating from frozen lakes, but this was short-lived.

The German assault on France and the Low Countries on 10 May put an end to the 'phoney war'. The RAF gave maximum support against the advancing German columns but, in the face of overwhelming odds, its efforts were to little avail. By the end of May the remaining aircraft and personnel had been withdrawn to Britain:

> The news from France is very bad … We have become the sole champions now in arms to defend the world cause. We shall do our best to be worthy of this honour. We shall defend our island home, and with the British Empire we shall fight on unconquerable until the curse of Hitler is lifted from the brows of mankind.
>
> **Winston Churchill**, 17 June 1940

2 JULY

Hitler told it would take four days to remove fighter protection from southern England and three weeks to destroy the RAF: Luftflotte II under Field Marshal Kesselring to operate east of a line Le Havre–Solent–Oxford–Birmingham–Manchester and Luftflotte III under Field Marshal Speerle to the west. Luftflotte V, under General Stumpf, to tackle northern England and Scotland, and fly diversions. Widespread anti-shipping operations to wear down the RAF. About 3,500 aircraft available.

10 JULY

The air battle commences: This day is considered by senior RAF officers to have been the start of the Battle of Britain. Fighter Command had fifty-two squadrons, in three groups (Nos 11–13 Groups). There were 199 Spitfires with nineteen squadrons, 347 Hurricanes across twenty-five squadrons, two squadrons with twenty-five Defiants and six with a total of sixty-nine Blenheim night fighters. This provided 640 aircraft with 1,456 pilots for operations. A westbound convoy was attacked off Folkestone by twenty Do17s, escorted by thirty Bf110s and twenty Bf109s. Fighter Command flew 609 sorties, losing six aircraft, while thirteen German aircraft failed to return. South Wales was raided by lone Ju88s.

Hurricane Is, like these lined up with No. 111 Squadron at Northolt in 1939, equipped the majority of the RAF's fighter squadrons in the first year of the war.

Spitfires and Hurricanes, operating from airfields in Kent, Surrey and Sussex, covered the evacuation from Dunkirk, which enabled the bulk of the British Expeditionary Force to be brought across the Channel in a flotilla of boats. But 944 RAF aircraft were lost in the Battle for France between 10 May and 20 June 1940, including 386 Hurricanes and sixty-seven Spitfires. Fortunately Air Chief Marshal Sir Hugh Dowding, the Commander-in-Chief of Fighter Command, had been successful in refusing to send further fighter squadrons to France; these reserves proved to be essential in the forthcoming Battle of Britain. The Luftwaffe had not got off lightly either. The campaign through May and June 1940 cost some 900 aircraft on operations, including 200 Messerschmitt Bf109Es, 100 Bf110s and a similar number of Junkers Ju87 dive-bombers, and almost 500 medium bombers.

What General Weygand has called the Battle of France is over …
The Battle of Britain is about to begin. Upon this battle depends the
survival of Christian civilisation. Upon it depends our own British
life, and the long continuity of our institutions and our Empire.

Winston Churchill, 18 June 1940

The Spitfire, seen here landing at Duxford painted in No. 19 Squadron markings, played an increasingly important part in the
Battle of Britain in its later stages as its performance improved.

11 JULY

Convoy dive-bombed
in Lyme Bay, Dorset. At
6 p.m. He111s delivered
the first large-scale
raid on a British city –
Portsmouth – where
seventeen people were
killed and fifty injured.
The Luftwaffe lost eleven
aircraft and the RAF four
in the course of 432
sorties.

15 JULY

Westland Aircraft factory at Yeovil bombed in daylight; Avonmouth and St Athan were also attacked.

Two Junkers Ju87B Stukas returning to their base in France after attacking shipping.

Commander-in-Chief of RAF Fighter Command throughout the Battle of Britain was Air Chief Marshal Sir Hugh Dowding.

2 GERMANY ATTACKS – BRITAIN DEFENDS

U p to mid 1940 the German military might had proved invincible in its rampage across Western Europe, and the invasion fleets were massed and waiting on the other side of the Channel. Germany needed to secure a beachhead on the English coast to bring the huge invading army ashore. But the crossing would be dangerous, being open to air attack, so the plan was to destroy the RAF, just as other air forces in Europe had been destroyed by blitzkrieg from September 1939 to May 1940. Then, with air superiority assured, the Luftwaffe's bomber force would have been used to support a cross-Channel invasion of southern England (Operation *Sea Lion*). Hitler monitored developments day by day, ready to give the order as soon as the skies were clear.

Luftwaffe bombers make a daylight attack on a convoy in the Straits of Dover.

15 JULY

Hitler issued a directive which began: 'Since England, in spite of her hopeless military situation, shows no sign of being ready to come to an understanding, I have decided to prepare a landing operation against England and, if necessary, carry it out.'

18 JULY

Following unopposed Luftwaffe bombing of Swansea and Falmouth, No. 10 Group became operational in south-west England with four squadrons of Hurricanes and four of Spitfires.

The Luftwaffe's bombing strategy was first concentrated on shipping in the English Channel.

Before the German Army could land, the Luftwaffe had first to destroy British coastal convoys, sink or immobilise the Royal Navy and above all ground the RAF. Airfields had to be bombed to render them impossible for aircraft to take off and land – and the RAF's dwindling number of fighters had to be destroyed while they were still on the ground.

There were five phases to the famous battle in the sky. Phase 1 lasted through the first month from 10 July to 7 August, with the Luftwaffe concentrating on shipping in the English Channel. This was an assault on Britain's lifeline; it was also an attempt to draw the RAF's fighters out over the sea so that pilots shot down were less likely to survive.

During Phase 2 (8–18 August) and Phase 3 (19 August–6 September) the aim was to destroy RAF Fighter Command on the ground and in the air. The full strength of the Luftwaffe was hurled at RAF airfields and aircraft. On 15 August, the Luftwaffe launched its main attack, *Eagle Day*, that was designed as the great knockout blow, but it turned out to be a disaster. The Luftwaffe lost seventy-five aircraft, the RAF thirty in the air (and another twenty-four on the ground). The last weeks of August and the first week of September proved the crucial time for the RAF, as during this period Germany finally got its priorities correct and went for the whole structure of Fighter Command – the airfields, radar stations and control centres.

Between 8 August and 6 September Fighter Command lost 210 aircrew and no fewer than 462 aircraft. It was a visibly wasting asset, and worse than the number of pilots lost was the pervading weariness of both pilots and ground crew, especially those in No. 11 Group. Worst of all, and no doubt largely due to stress, was the loss of seasoned pilots and leaders. By 7 September, one in five of Dowding's squadron commanders had been killed or wounded. This drove Britain's air defence to the very edge of collapse.

Fighter Command suffered a heavy toll of aircrew and aircraft in August 1940.

19 JULY

Nine newly arrived Defiants of No. 141 Squadron took off from RAF Hawkinge on their first patrol but were decimated by twenty Bf109s when defending Dover from a Junkers Ju87 Stuka attack. Five of the Defiants were lost and two badly damaged before the arrival of No. 111 Squadron Hurricanes. Only three pilots and one gunner survived from the seven aircraft.

3 HEIGHT OF THE BATTLE

The gratitude of every home in our Island, in our Empire and indeed throughout the world, except in the abodes of the guilty, goes out to the British airmen, who, undaunted by odds, unwearied in their constant challenge and mortal danger, are turning the tide of world war by their prowess and by their devotion. Never in the field of human conflict was so much owed by so many to so few. All hearts go out to the fighter pilots, whose brilliant actions we see with our own eyes day after day.

Winston Churchill, House of Commons, 20 August 1940

On 7 September, Luftwaffe Commander-in-Chief Reichsmarschall Hermann Göring threw victory away, ordering the Luftwaffe to switch targets. Believing the exaggerated claims of his pilots, he had decided the British were already finished. Had the RAF been beaten in the air, everything else would have followed as a matter of course. He prematurely moved on to Phase 4 – the attempt to crush Britain's will to resist by shattering attacks on London and other major cities – which lasted until 5 October. Air Chief Marshal Sir Hugh Dowding, Commander-in-Chief of Fighter Command and responsible for

20 JULY

The RAF had 609 single-engined fighters on strength with 531 serviceable on this day. The Luftwaffe had 1,055 Bf109 and Bf110 fighters with 824 operational.

Spitfire pilots scramble as their airfield comes under attack by Luftwaffe bombers.

No. 609 Squadron Spitfire IA R6915 flown by F/O John Dundas, shooting down a Luftwaffe Messerschmitt Bf110 in August 1940. (Artwork by Wilfred Hardy, GAvA)

25 JULY

Stukas bombed Portland and Do17s attacked convoy CW8 off Dover, sinking five ships. Ju87 Stukas scored hits on destroyer HMS *Boreas*. This was the most hectic day so far, with six Spitfires lost and four pilots killed.

26 JULY

No. 54 Squadron flew its Spitfire Is to RAF Catterick for rest after 504 sorties (800 hours) in three weeks and twelve aircraft lost. It was replaced at Hornchurch by No. 41 Squadron.

Heinkel He111s provided the Luftwaffe's main heavy bomber strength.

In September 1940 the Luftwaffe delivered its heaviest bombing attacks on London.

home defence, ordered every available fighter within 60 miles of London to the Thames Estuary. Early that evening, one of the greatest air battles was fought above the Isle of Sheppey when some 300 RAF fighters tackled 900 German fighters and bombers. Both sides suffered heavily; forty-one German aircraft were destroyed, but the Luftwaffe broke through to bomb the East End of London.

London was burning and, as the sun set, the flames in the East End could be seen from central London, providing a beacon for the Luftwaffe to find its target through until dawn the following day. The fires continued to burn and the bombers returned the next night. On 15 September 1940, a day now remembered as Battle of Britain Day, Göring launched another massive attack, with 1,000 sorties flown against London. The resulting encounter was tense and complex. That evening the people were told that 185 German aircraft had been shot down and a great victory won.

27 JULY

Ju87 Stukas attacked a convoy off Swanage, Dorset and also made two raids on Dover. Destroyer HMS *Wren* was sunk off Aldeburgh by He111s. Twenty-eight fighter squadrons were then defending the south-east of England.

Messerschmitt Bf109E 'White 9' crashed in a field near Ramsgate in August 1940.

The sky over Britain was pencilled with white vapour trails, with occasional angry puffs of smoke smearing the clear blue of a perfect English summer. This was the scene, set to the drone of aircraft engines, the menacing bark of anti-aircraft fire and the roar of machine guns, which became commonplace during the Battle of Britain.

The Times

During the hard-fought actions on the 15th, the Luftwaffe actually lost fifty-eight aircraft, as against the thirty-one lost by RAF Fighter Command. Although the German losses fell far short of the number claimed destroyed by the defences at the time, there can be no doubt that the day's fighting decided the outcome of the battle. Fighter Command was still stoically in business and the German High Command could see that it was not going to be beaten before the weather broke in the autumn.

Luftwaffe Commander-in-Chief Reichsmarschall Hermann Göring addressing a group of pilots.

That was the day Göering had said to his pilots the RAF is down to its last 50 Spitfires. But they ran up against 23 squadrons for a start when they were on their way in, and when they got over London, with the Messerschmitt 109s running out of fuel, in comes Douglas Bader with 60 more fighters, and got stuck in.

Fight of the Few

The importance of Dowding's use of radar information to plot the incoming Luftwaffe raiders on a large tabletop map and from this direct their interception by RAF fighters should not be underestimated.

Hermann Göring, the Luftwaffe supremo, had no doubt about its ability to destroy the RAF and thought it could be achieved in a matter of days or weeks. His view was supported by German air intelligence. How did they get it so wrong and bring about the first major setback for Germany in the Second World War? Apart from the dogged determination of the British Hurricane and Spitfire pilots and the qualities of their aircraft, the main miscalculation was not appreciating the use being made by the fighter controllers of the radar equipment around the coast. Integrating this with the reports coming in from observers on the ground, information on the incoming bombers was quickly passed on so that the fighters could be scrambled and sent directly to attack the Heinkels, Dorniers and Junkers without spending time searching for them.

27/28 JULY
Night raid on Belfast. Fighter engagements over the Channel coast.

4 INVASION CANCELLED

On 17 September 1940 Hitler ordered that Operation *Sea Lion*, the planned invasion of southern England, be postponed until further notice. The ships and barges concentrated at ports along the Channel coast started to disperse and the threat of invasion diminished with each day that passed. The Battle of Britain would run for a few more weeks, but its outcome had been decided. The Luftwaffe was redirected to switch to the night-time 'blitz' on London and other cities in Phase 5, which lasted until the end of October.

29 JULY

Four very large Luftwaffe fighter formations protected Ju87 Stukas dive-bombing Dover Harbour. With many lone bombers operating, several Channel convoys were attacked and HMS *Delight* was sunk off Portland.

Biggest of the Luftwaffe's bombers, the Heinkel He111 carried up to 4,000lb of bombs in its fuselage bomb bay.

The price of victory in the Battle of Britain was not achieved without cost. Of the 3,080 aircrew (2,543 from the UK and the remainder from Poland, New Zealand, Canada, Czechoslovakia, Belgium, South Africa, Australia, Free France, Eire, USA, Southern Rhodesia, Jamaica and Palestine) who fought in the battle, 537 (including 375 pilots) were killed and many more were wounded. Fighter Command lost 915 aircraft from a total of 1,017 RAF and Fleet Air Arm losses, whilst the Luftwaffe suffered the loss of 1,733 bombers and fighters. The aircraft factories continued to function day and night and managed to keep pace with losses, introducing new versions of the Spitfire (Mark II) and Hurricane (Mark IIA) at the height of the battle. Fighter Command had won the Battle of Britain, but Bomber Command still had the task of taking the war to the enemy's homeland.

A Heinkel He111H heading across London on 7 September 1940 to drop its eight 250kg bombs onto the Surrey and West India Docks.

30 JULY

Hitler directed that the Luftwaffe should prepare immediately for 'the great air battle against England'.

Fire tenders on the River Thames spray water onto the burning dockside warehouses.

30 & 31 JULY

Combat losses: Luftwaffe: 151 aircraft missing, 58 written off, 52 seriously damaged. RAF total losses (UK-based aircraft): 154 missing, 69 written off, 59 seriously damaged. Overall losses included 62 Hurricanes, 60 Spitfires, 18 Blenheims, 23 Hampdens, 12 Wellingtons and 10 Whitleys.

The Battle of Britain was not just a fight between Hurricanes and Heinkels, Spitfires and Messerschmitts. Nor was it some contest between Adolf Galland and a British counterpart. It really did involve the entire nation. The 'we' who were going to 'fight them on the beaches' and 'never surrender' was all of the British people, confirmed when bombs struck homes nationwide and not just on the south-east, although in the summer of 1940 that area was at the heart of a ferocious battle.

Had the Battle of Britain gone the other way, the whole future of the world could have been changed dramatically. With Britain invaded and the threat to his west neutralised, Hitler would have turned all his attention and his vast resources eastwards. America may not have come into the war in Europe, and the German advance eastward and southward might eventually have met up with the Japanese, leaving the Axis powers 'masters of the globe'.

5 DUXFORD – SPITFIRES AND THE BIG WING

Thursday 4 August 1938 saw an event that ensured RAF Duxford, Cambridge, a place in aviation history. On that afternoon the third production Spitfire, K9789, already overdue for delivery to the RAF, was ready for its final factory test. Supermarine's test pilot Jeffrey Quill decided that if all was well he would stay airborne and fly the aircraft straight to No. 19 Squadron at Duxford. There were no snags and he was there within forty minutes. Duxford's and No. 19 Squadron's operational record books have identical entries for 4 August 1938: 'First Spitfire for intensive flying on re-equipment'.

On 12 August a second Spitfire, K9790, arrived for intensive flying with No. 66 Squadron. The two squadrons were required to reach 400 hours on the aircraft as soon as possible and by 22 September K9789 had reached 240 hours in forty-two days, an average of around five and a half hours a day. During October Spitfire deliveries to No. 19 Squadron got under way, and by the end of 1938 both squadrons were up to strength and operational on type.

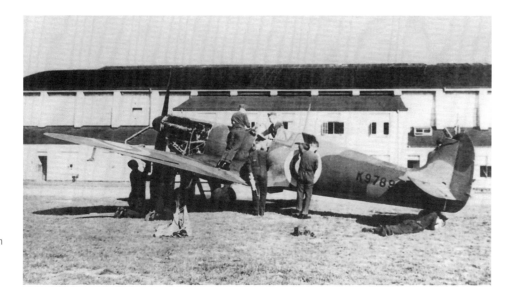

K9789, the third production Spitfire I, at Duxford in August 1938.

1–11 AUGUST
Bad weather resulted in much reduced operations. 5,800 high explosives (HEs) were known to have fallen so far. Convoys were still attacked, as were Dover and Portland harbours.

Line up of No. 19 Squadron's new Spitfire Is at RAF Duxford on 4 May 1939.

1 AUGUST

Boulton & Paul aircraft factory at Norwich was bombed. German propaganda leaflets entitled *A Last Appeal to Reason* were widely scattered over Britain by the Luftwaffe.

Spitfire training continued into 1939 and, as the summer wore on, tension mounted. After war was declared, both squadrons flew daily patrols from RAF Horsham St Faith, Norfolk, over the North Sea for shipping and fishing fleet protection. They were joined by the Blenheim IFs of the newly formed No. 222 Squadron in November.

On 11 January 1940, Duxford-based squadrons were involved in their first action of the war. No. 66 Squadron was scrambled from Horsham St Faith to catch a Luftwaffe Heinkel He111 which had attacked a trawler. Three Spitfires intercepted it, damaging the port engine. The Heinkel was then lost in cloud and the No. 66 Squadron fighters returned to base, but the enemy aircraft was later reported to have crashed in Denmark. On 7 February, No. 19 Squadron welcomed back Douglas Bader who, at the outbreak of war, had argued his way back into the RAF. While the squadron was temporarily at RAF Horsham St Faith, Bader had some problems getting used to Spitfires and suffered a take-off accident. The Spitfire cartwheeled and was written off, as were Bader's artificial legs, but he carried on flying with a new pair. In April, No. 222 Squadron exchanged its Blenheims for Spitfires.

Newly equipped with Blenheim Is, No. 222 Squadron arrived at Duxford in November 1939.

When No. 222 Squadron re-equipped with Spitfire Is in April 1940, the legendary Flight Lieutenant Douglas Bader (*centre*) became a flight commander.

In May 1940, Bader became No. 222 Squadron's flight commander and left Duxford when the squadron was replaced by No. 264 Squadron equipped with Boulton Paul Defiants. Enemy encounters were now happening regularly and on 11 May Flight Lieutenant W.G. Clouston claimed No. 19 Squadron's first victory, a Junkers Ju88. With the resident Duxford squadrons having temporarily moved away to fly patrols over Dunkirk for the British Expeditionary Force, No. 92 Squadron's Spitfires provided local cover. During this ten-day period No. 19 Squadron met the Luftwaffe on five occasions, claiming twenty-eight victories but losing three aircraft. No. 264 Squadron suffered considerably in May, claiming fifty-six victories but losing fourteen aircraft. The turreted Defiant was no longer a surprise to an expectant enemy and the squadron was stood down at Duxford.

By June 1940, Holland, Belgium and France having fallen to Hitler's forces, an attack on Britain seemed imminent. The night of 5 June saw the first night bombing raid on England, and the next night raiders came into the Cambridge and Duxford area. No. 19 Squadron began to fly night patrols to ward them off, but with little success. On 25 June, No. 19 Squadron moved to Fowlmere, Duxford's main satellite airfield, positioned 3 miles away. This made room for a new squadron, No. 310, to be formed with Hurricanes. They were flown mainly by Czechoslovakian pilots who, Hitler's troops

Defiant I day fighters of No. 264 Squadron, based at Duxford and Fowlmere from May to July 1940.

2 AUGUST

A lone Luftwaffe raider attempted to bomb the Forth Bridge in Scotland.

The Junkers Ju88, a fast medium bomber that was also capable of dive-bombing.

having invaded their own country, had joined the French Air Force only to then end up joining the RAF after France's fall.

The German High Command held the view that Luftwaffe air supremacy was key to the successful invasion of Britain. To achieve this, the RAF had to be destroyed. The essential strategy involved bombing RAF airfields and tasking the escorting fighters with any retaliatory action needed. The period of intense air fighting that followed brought raids on the airfields in the south-east, gradually nearing Duxford, and by the end of July enemy air activity was almost constant.

August was another busy month, with regular day- and night-time patrols. Duxford was a sector station in No. 12 Group, tasked with defending the Midlands, and called in to help No. 11 Group at times of maximum effort. No. 11 Group, defending London and the south-east of England, bore the brunt of the fighting, and it was thought that some sort of reserve could help when times were hardest. Three Duxford Sector squadrons, 19, 310 and 611, were available and ready to assist No. 11 Group if requested. The scale of fighting over Kent and Surrey on 30 August was such that the air officer commanding No. 12 Group, Air Vice Marshal Trafford Leigh-Mallory, decided that Duxford should host an additional readily deployable squadron. Coltishall's Hurricane-equipped

3 AUGUST
The first Spitfire IIAs were delivered to No. 611 Squadron at RAF Digby.

Czech pilots of No. 310 Squadron on the grass at Duxford, in front of Hurricane I P3143.

5 AUGUST

Hitler suggested that the RAF 'should be destroyed today!' The second phase of the Battle of Britain began, with the intensification of Luftwaffe bombing.

No. 242 Squadron, now commanded by Squadron Leader Douglas Bader, therefore arrived to join Nos 19 and 310 Squadrons on daily standby. Almost immediately, the Bader-led No. 242 Squadron was ordered to cover North Weald, a No. 11 Group sector station about 30 miles south of Duxford, when an attacking force of Heinkel He111s and Messerschmitt Bf110s appeared from the east heading for the north London suburb of Enfield. Unseen by the enemy pilots, No. 242 Squadron attacked down-sun, claiming twelve victories.

As a leading proponent of the 'big wing' concept, Bader was convinced that the most effective fighter tactic involved a single strike force combining several squadrons. Leigh-Mallory strongly supported him, though his No. 11 Group counterpart, Air Vice Marshal Keith R. Park, did not. Park argued that to assemble a 'big wing' would consume too much valuable combat time. This controversy caused a serious rift between them.

Luftwaffe Dornier Do17s, escorted by Messerschmitt Bf110s, attacked the Duxford Sector and bombed No. 19 Squadron's Fowlmere base on 31 August. No. 19 Squadron intercepted the raiders,

Squadron Leader Douglas Bader, commanding officer of
No. 242 Squadron, poses (*centre*) with pilots in front of a
Hurricane at Duxford in August 1940.

Air Vice Marshal Trafford Leigh-Mallory, air officer commanding
No. 12 Group.

8 AUGUST

Luftwaffe practice day
for 'that big blow'. Three
raids on CW9 'Peewit'
convoy, which had been
discovered by German
radar near Dover during
darkness, and an E-Boat
attack followed. Ju87
Stukas attacked two
convoys. Fierce fighting
ensued and twenty
German aircraft were
shot down. No. 145
Squadron (Hurricanes)
claimed ten, but lost
five pilots. The RAF lost
twenty-two fighters and
seven ships were sunk;
four managed to reach
Swanage.

Air Vice Marshal Keith Park, air officer commanding No. 11 Group, in his 'personal' Hurricane.

11 AUGUST

150 raiders approached Portland behind a naval smoke screen and installations were seriously damaged. There were night raids on the ports of Bristol, Cardiff and Middlesborough. Heavy fighting cost the Luftwaffe thirty-five aircraft (including thirteen Bf109s and 10 Bf110s). Fighter Command lost thirty-one aircraft.

and destroyed two enemy aircraft. Two Spitfires were lost, but both pilots involved baled out to safety. However, 19-year-old Pilot Officer Ray Aeberhardt was killed trying to land his damaged Spitfire back at Fowlmere. All three squadrons (Nos 19, 242 and 310) were still acting under individual orders, and later that same day No. 310 Squadron saw its first action, attacking a formation of Dornier Do17/215s, escorted by Messerschmitt Bf109s and Bf110s, east of Hornchurch. Its aircraft claimed four Dorniers and one Bf109, damaging a further two. Two Hurricanes were lost but one pilot was saved.

During the morning of 3 September, Nos 19 and 310 Squadrons intercepted a large Luftwaffe force that had bombed North Weald and claimed eight enemy aircraft destroyed, and one probable. One of No. 310 Squadron's Hurricanes was lost but its pilot was saved, and No. 19 Squadron's commanding officer Squadron Leader Pinkham's cannon jammed. In the afternoon, the head of Fighter Command, Air Chief Marshal Dowding flew in to Duxford without warning and addressed No. 19 Squadron about this recurring cannon problem. Consequently, that same evening, the cannon Spitfires were removed and eight machine-gun-equipped Spitfires were delivered to Fowlmere.

Squadron Leader Pinkham led No. 19 Squadron on patrol over Hornchurch on 5 September and encountered an enemy force consisting of forty Dornier Do17s escorted by forty Messerschmitt Bf109s. Contrary to popular belief, when attacked by fighters the Luftwaffe bomber formations seldom split up, because of the mutual fire support achieved by retaining a cohesive formation. One such formation shot down Squadron Leader Pinkham, and he was killed baling out too close to the ground. Flight Lieutenant Brian Lane replaced him, becoming No. 19 Squadron's fourth commanding officer in nine months.

On 6 September, No. 19 Squadron was ordered to fly in a wing with Nos 242 and 310 Squadrons, Bader's 'big wing' idea had become reality. The Duxford Wing's first launch involved RAF Hornchurch and North Weald patrols, but had no encounters with enemy aircraft. Saturday 7 September saw the Luftwaffe's first major daylight attack on London and in Britain the code name *Cromwell* was broadcast: 'invasion imminent'. All twenty-one squadrons of No. 11 Group became airborne, stretching it to the limit. No. 12 Group's assistance was requested and, under Bader's unofficial leadership, the Duxford Wing took off, heading for RAF Debden and North Weald. Fighting was fierce and, by the day's end, Luftwaffe aircraft losses totalled forty.

No. 611 Squadron's Spitfires arrived to join No. 19 Squadron at Fowlmere in the Duxford Sector on 8 September. The squadron was not absorbed into the wing but instead provided a local defensive precaution or extra reinforcement. The Duxford Wing was again ordered into action on 9 September. A formation of about seventy-five Dornier Do17/215s and about 150 Messerschmitt Bf109, Bf110 and Heinkel He111 escorts were sighted south of the Thames Estuary

A No. 19 Squadron Spitfire I being rearmed at Fowlmere.

12 AUGUST

There were seven distinct operations: Bf109 sweeps followed by very damaging Bf110 attacks on four south coast radar stations; a heavy midday raid on Portsmouth; Ju88s dropped seventy-two HEs, disastrously savaging Ventnor, Isle of Wight, radar; first raids made on British fighter airfields; Bf110s attacked RAF Manston, Kent, followed by Do17s 'carpet bombing'; two Ju87 Stuka attacks were made on a convoy before heavy raids on Hawkinge and Lympne in the late afternoon; and Bf109 fighters attacked Dunkirk, Kent, radar station. The RAF flew 196 patrols (798 sorties) losing twenty-two fighters, while the Luftwaffe mounted 1,200 sorties, losing twenty-six aircraft.

13 AUGUST

'Eagle Day' (*Adler Tag*), the opening day of major Luftwaffe attacks on England, which had been postponed from 10 August because of poor weather. It began with Do17s attacking Coastal Command's Eastchurch, Fairey Battle anti-invasion base. With more good weather in the late afternoon, forty Junkers Ju88s headed for Southampton and RAF Middle Wallop. The latter raid went astray. Junkers Ju87 Stukas found Rochford and others devastated RAF Detling killing sixty-seven personnel. The Luftwaffe lost forty-four aircraft. Fighter Command flew 727 sorties and lost fourteen aircraft with seven pilots killed. Night targets included Castle Bromwich and Shorts at Belfast, where five new Stirlings were destroyed.

Alongside the He111, the slower Dornier Do17 was the Luftwaffe's main bomber during the Battle of Britain.

A Heinkel He111, one of the many German bombers that crash-landed in southern England after being damaged by RAF fighters.

heading north-west. Two No. 19 Squadron Spitfires were damaged and two No. 310 Squadron Hurricanes were destroyed after colliding, the pilot of one was killed; No. 242 Squadron also lost two fighters and one pilot was killed. That day's Luftwaffe aircraft losses totalled twenty-seven. After the action, which had progressed well south of Duxford, the wing's aircraft, low on fuel, were scattered and landed at various No. 11 Group airfields. Until the wing had reassembled at Duxford, refuelled and rearmed, it could not operate as a 'wing at readiness'.

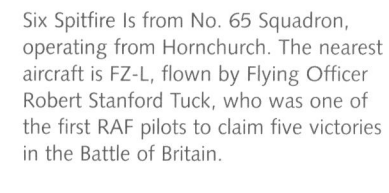

Six Spitfire Is from No. 65 Squadron, operating from Hornchurch. The nearest aircraft is FZ-L, flown by Flying Officer Robert Stanford Tuck, who was one of the first RAF pilots to claim five victories in the Battle of Britain.

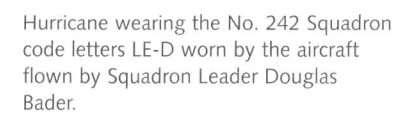

Hurricane wearing the No. 242 Squadron code letters LE-D worn by the aircraft flown by Squadron Leader Douglas Bader.

14 AUGUST

Less activity that day; 500 Luftwaffe sorties were mounted, including a Bf110 low-level Manston raid, but only four 250kg bombs were actually dropped on the airfield. Two Ju87 Stukas raids on Dover were mostly driven off. Small-scale attacks on Middle Wallop, Hullavington and Kemble airfields. He111s bombed Portland.

15 AUGUST

Eight major attacks on airfields. Ju87 Stukas raided Hawkinge, Folkestone and Lympne. Heinkels made a feint towards Montrose, then seventy-two Norway-based He111s and thirty-five Bf110s headed for Driffield and Linton-on-Ouse airfields but made a wrong landfall near the Farne Islands. Surprised to be intercepted, they released their bombs on Seaham Harbour. A second force, fifty KG30 Ju88s from Denmark, bombed Driffield; twelve Whitleys and five hangars were damaged. RAF fighter interception successes (possibly twenty-four) showed the Luftwaffe the extent of British fighter effectiveness and the danger of inadequate escort. Tough afternoon fighting followed over Rochester as Do17s tried to bomb the Short and Pobjoy factories.

➤

Dornier Do17 of Kampfgeshwader 76, with its bomb doors open and starboard engine on fire, shortly before it crashed at Hurst Green, Kent. It had been shot down by a Kenley-based Hurricane I of No. 32 Squadron.

An increasing number of Luftwaffe bombers like this Dornier Do17Z fell victim to the defending Spitfires and Hurricanes during the first two weeks of September.

Squadron Leader Douglas Bader flew to No. 12 Group HQ at Hucknall on 10 September, where he and Air Vice Marshal Leigh-Mallory discussed the wing's progress to date and considered future possibilities. Led by Squadron Leader A.G. 'Sailor' Malan, No. 74 Squadron's Spitfires flew to Fowlmere to join with Nos 19 and 611 Squadrons. Leigh-Mallory's reinforcement policy continued with the arrival at Duxford of No. 302 Squadron, comprised of Polish pilots flying Hurricanes. Now there were some fifty or sixty fighters dispersed around Duxford and Fowlmere. Late on 11 September, an all-Spitfire

wing consisting of Nos 19, 74, 266 and 611 Squadrons' aircraft attacked a large Luftwaffe bomber formation south-east of London, claiming thirteen enemy aircraft destroyed and five damaged for the loss of two Spitfires and one pilot.

On 15 September the reason for the preceding days' lull became clear. On what is now known as Battle of Britain Day, the aerial combat reached its climax. At 11.30 a.m. the Duxford Wing, comprising Nos 19, 242, 302 and 310 Squadrons, was scrambled and joined by No. 611 Squadron from Digby. The wing ran into what Flight Lieutenant Brian Lane later described as 'the whole Luftwaffe' over London. Intense combat followed, from Dungeness in the east to Kingston-upon-Thames in the west. The Duxford Wing reportedly destroyed fifteen of the fifty-six Luftwaffe aircraft lost, itself losing three Hurricanes and two Spitfires. Duxford was cock-a-hoop, and Fighter Command had won the battle for London, by day at least.

The Duxford Wing was back in action on 18 September. After two uneventful earlier sorties, the wing, again comprising Nos 19, 242, 302, 310 and 611 Squadrons, took to the air and intercepted

A formation of twenty-four Luftwaffe Dornier Do17Zs en route to bomb south-east England.

Portland was again targeted, while Ju88s attacked Southampton and Middle Wallop. An intended Biggin Hill raid turned into a West Malling attack. Early evening saw Bf110s bomb Croydon Aerodrome, possibly mistaking it for Kenley. On what was dubbed 'Black Thursday' the Luftwaffe suffered its worst losses in a single day of the battle. Nearly 2,000 Luftwaffe sorties were flown during which sixty-nine aircraft and 190 aircrew were lost while RAF Fighter Command flew 974 sorties, losing thirty-four aircraft and thirteen pilots. The average RAF fighter squadron now had nineteen pilots. In the twenty-four hours ending at 6 a.m. on 16 August, 867 HEs listed as falling on the UK killed seventy-nine civilians, with 196 seriously injured.

16 AUGUST

In a two-pronged afternoon attack, West Malling airfield was bombed but a Hornchurch raid was driven off, so Tilbury and Northfleet were bombed instead. Ju87 Stukas seriously damaged RAF Tangmere. Ventnor radar station was hit as well as three hangars at Lee-on-Solent. Ju88s bombed Gosport, causing a hangar fire. A late afternoon raid on the Vickers factory at Brooklands by He111s was driven off – but the bombers unloaded on the Wimbledon and Mitcham areas. Probable first combat success by an RAF cannon-armed fighter, a Spitfire of No. 19 Squadron, off Harwich. Two Ju88s destroyed forty-six Oxfords of No. 2 SFTS and other aircraft in a hangar at RAF Brize Norton. The Luftwaffe flew 1,700 sorties, losing

➤

Badly damaged hangars at RAF Middle Wallop after a Luftwaffe raid.

two unescorted bomber formations, made up of between twenty and thirty enemy aircraft each, over the Thames at Gravesend. The wing shot down six Ju88s with only two of its aircraft damaged in the engagement. This was the Luftwaffe's last attempted large-formation raid on Britain. During the next few days the Duxford Wing patrolled without encountering serious action.

On 25 September, the Poles of 302 Squadron left Duxford and No. 616 Squadron replaced No. 611 Squadron. The wing (242, 310 and 616 Squadrons) was scrambled on 26 September and again on the 27th when it became engaged in the heaviest fighting encountered for some time in the Dover–Canterbury area. The wing *claimed* twenty-one enemy aircraft destroyed – its own losses were four aircraft, plus two pilots killed and one wounded. With now just the three original squadrons (19, 242 and 310) remaining at Duxford and Fowlmere, and Luftwaffe daylight raids dying down, the 'big wing' essentially passed into history. By October's end, the Luftwaffe made few daylight raids, though night-time attacks persisted. From November, Duxford squadrons flew offensive patrols over France and added shipping protection sorties to the daily workload. RAF Fighter Command had been successful, the threat of invasion had passed, and Duxford's squadrons and its controversial 'big wing' had played an important part in winning the Battle of Britain.

6 THE BATTLE OF BRITAIN VC

Twenty-one Victoria Crosses (VCs) were awarded to the RAF in the Second World War, but only one VC – the highest decoration for valour – was awarded to a fighter pilot during the Battle of Britain. Flight Lieutenant James Brindley Nicolson was the sole member of Fighter Command to be so honoured.

Nicolson had joined the RAF in December 1936 and was serving with No. 72 Squadron at the outbreak of war. He was posted to No. 249 Squadron at RAF Church Fenton in May 1940, and as 'A' Flight Commander he moved south with the squadron to Boscombe Down on 14 August 1940. The battle was at its height and No. 249 Squadron found itself in the thick of the fighting. Equipped with Hawker Hurricane Is, it was responsible for the protection of central southern England, guarding the skies over Wiltshire, Hampshire and Dorset.

The Victoria Cross awarded to Flight Lieutenant James Nicolson in November 1940.

Flt Lt James Nicolson, the only Fighter Command pilot to be awarded the VC during the Battle of Britain.

forty-five aircraft, while the RAF lost twenty-five fighters. Flt Lt J.B. Nicolson, flying Hurricane P3576 of No. 249 Squadron, fought on in the blazing fighter before baling out. He was later awarded the Victoria Cross, and was the only Battle of Britain fighter pilot to receive this, the highest honour for valour.

Two days after the squadron's arrival, Red Section was dispatched on a patrol over the Poole, Ringwood and Salisbury areas. Nicolson led the section in Hurricane P3576 and was accompanied by Squadron Leader Eric King and Pilot Officer Martyn King into action against an attacking force of Messerschmitt Bf110s and Junkers Ju88s bent on destroying Gosport. As Nicolson turned to attack the invaders, his section was itself attacked by Messerschmitt Bf109s. All three defenders were hit.

Nicolson and fellow officers at the RAF convalescent home at Torquay.

Nicolson with his mother, wife Muriel and two sisters shortly after he received the Victoria Cross on 25 November.

Squadron Leader King was able to get his Hurricane back to Boscombe Down, although it was badly damaged. The other two were not so lucky. Pilot Officer King baled out of his aircraft, but his parachute collapsed on the descent and he suffered fatal injuries.

Nicolson's Hurricane was hit by four cannon shells, two of which wounded him while another set fire to the fuel gravity tank. As he was about to bale out of the fighter because of the flames in his cockpit, he saw an enemy aircraft. This he attacked and shot down, although as a result of staying in the aircraft he sustained serious burns to his hands, face, neck and legs. His ordeal was not over, for on his parachute descent he was buzzed by a Luftwaffe fighter, but he feigned death so was not shot at.

On reaching the ground safely he was taken to the Royal Southampton Hospital, where it was found that he had third-degree burns to the whole of his body from the waist down and on his hands.

James Nicolson was awarded the Victoria Cross for 'exceptional gallantry and disregard for the safety of his own life'. Shortly after the Battle of Britain the announcement appeared in the *London Gazette*, and he was invested by King George VI nine days later.

17 AUGUST

No. 1 RCAF Squadron became operational. Since 8 August, ninety-four RAF fighter pilots had been killed and sixty-five seriously wounded. The serious drain on fighter pilot resources was recognised by the Air Ministry. Air Chief Marshal Dowding asked for and got volunteers from Battle and Lysander Squadrons to join Fighter Command.

18 AUGUST

Midday raid on RAF West Malling. Nine low-flying Do17s attacked Biggin Hill, with high-flying Ju88s following. Nearby RAF Kenley was similarly bombed. Two Dorniers were brought down by parachute and cable rocket devices. An afternoon dive-bomb attack on the radar station at Poling cost sixteen Ju87 Stukas shot down. Ford, Gosport and Thorney Island were also raided. In two weeks, thirty-nine Stukas had been destroyed. In the face of these heavy losses the Luftwaffe then withheld the remainder 'to support the invasion'. Two raids intended for Hornchurch and North Weald were driven off. The bombers had for the first time flown in over the Essex coast – a difficult and long route for the short-range Bf109 escorts. Night raids by between seventy and eighty aircraft continued.

COMBAT WITH A MESSERSCHMITT

Flight Lieutenant James Nicolson described, in a BBC broadcast in December 1940, his personal account of that dramatic combat with a Luftwaffe Messerschmitt Bf110 on 16 August 1940:

That day was a glorious day. The sun was shining from a cloudless sky and there was hardly a breath of wind anywhere. Our squadron was going towards Southampton on patrol at 15,000ft when I saw three Junkers 88 bombers about 4 miles away flying across our bows. I reported this to our squadron leader and he replied: 'Go after them with your section.' So I led my section of aircraft round towards the bombers. We chased hard after them, but when we were about a mile behind we saw the 88s fly straight into a squadron of Spitfires. I used to fly a Spitfire myself and I guessed it was curtains for the three Junkers. I was right and they were all shot down in quick time, with no pickings for us. I must confess I was very disappointed, for I had never fired at a Hun in my life and was longing to have a crack at them.

James Nicolson saw a trio of Junkers Ju88As, like these pictured here, destroyed by Spitfires.

So we swung round again and started to climb up to 18,000ft over Southampton, to rejoin our squadron. I was still a long way from the squadron when suddenly, very close in rapid succession, I heard four big bangs. They were the loudest noises I had ever heard and they had been made by four cannon shells from a Messerschmitt 110 hitting my machine.

The first shell tore through the hood over my cockpit and sent splinters into my left eye. One splinter, I discovered later, nearly severed my eyelid. I couldn't see through that eye for blood. The second cannon shell struck my petrol tank and set it on fire. The third shell crashed into the cockpit and tore off my right trouser leg.

The fourth shell struck the back of my left shoe. It shattered the heel of the shoe and made quite a mess of my left foot. But I didn't know anything about that, either, until later. Anyway, the effect of these four shells was to make me dive away to the right to avoid further shells. Then I started cursing myself for my carelessness. What a fool I had been, I thought, what a fool!

I was just thinking of jumping out when suddenly a Messerschmitt 110 whizzed under me and got right in my gunsights. Fortunately, no damage had been done to my windscreens or sights and when I was chasing the Junkers, I had switched everything on, so everything was set for a fight.

I pressed the gun button, for the Messerschmitt was in nice range; I plugged him first time and I could see my tracer bullets entering the German machine. He was going like mad, twisting and turning as he tried to get away from my fire. So I pushed the throttle wide open. Both of us must have been doing about 400mph as we went down together in a dive. First he turned left, then right, then left and right again. He did three turns to the right and finally a fourth turn to the left. I remember shouting out loud at him when I first saw him: 'I'll teach you some manners, you Hun,' and I shouted other things as well. I knew I was getting him nearly all the time I was firing.

By this time it was pretty hot inside my machine from the burst petrol tank. I couldn't see much flame, but I reckon it was there all right. I remember looking once at my left hand, which was keeping the throttle open. It seemed to be in the fire itself and I could see the skin peeling off it. Yet I had little pain. Unconsciously too, I had drawn my feet up under my parachute on the seat, to escape the heat, I suppose.

Well, I gave the Hun all I had and the last I saw of him was when he was going down, with his right wing lower than the left wing. I gave him a parting burst and, as he had disappeared, started thinking about saving myself. I decided it was time I left the aircraft and baled out, so I immediately jumped up from my seat. But first of all I hit my head against the framework of the hood, which was all that was left. I cursed myself for a fool, pulled the hood back (wasn't I relieved when it slid back beautifully) and jumped up again. Once again I bounced back into my seat, for I had forgotten to undo the straps holding me in. One of them snapped and so I only had one to undo. Then I left the machine.

I suppose I was about 12–15,000ft when I baled out. Immediately I started somersaulting downwards and after a few turns like that I found myself diving head first for the ground. After a second or two of this, I decided to pull the ripcord. The result was that I immediately straightened up and began to float down. Then an aircraft – a Messerschmitt, I think – came tearing past me. I decided to pretend I was dead and hung limply by the parachute straps. The Messerschmitt came back once, and I kept my eyes closed, but I didn't get the bullets I was half-expecting. I don't know if he fired at me; the main thing is that I wasn't hit.

19 AUGUST

Two Junkers Ju88s using only eight bombs set ablaze the Llanreith Pembroke Dock oil farm; it burnt for four days. East Anglian airfields were also attacked. He111s made a beam-controlled night raid on the Rolls-Royce factory at Derby.

Messerschmitt Bf110, similar to the fighter that shot down James Nicolson.

20 AUGUST

Attack on Southwold, and the Pembroke fire was further stoked. The night raid on Rolls-Royce at Derby was repeated. On this day Winston Churchill paid his tribute to Fighter Command with his famous words: 'Never, in the field of human conflict, was so much owed by so many to so few.'

While I was coming down like that I had a look at myself. I could see the bones of my left hand showing through the knuckles.

Then for the first time I discovered I'd been wounded in the foot. Blood was oozing out of the lace holes of my left boot. My right hand was pretty badly burned, too. So I hung down a bit longer and then decided to try my limbs, just to see if they would work – thank goodness they did. I still had my oxygen mask over my face, but my hands were in too bad a state to take it off. I tried to, but I couldn't manage it.

I found, too, that I had lost one trouser leg and the other was badly torn, and my tunic was just like a lot of torn rags, so I wasn't looking very smart. Then, after a bit more of this dangling down business, I began to ache all over and my hands and legs hurt a lot.

When I got lower, I saw I was in danger of coming down in the sea. I knew I didn't stand an earthly if I did, because I wouldn't have been able to swim a stroke with my hands like that. So I wriggled about a bit and managed to float inland. Then I saw a high-tension cable below me and thought it would finish me if I hit that. So I wriggled a bit more and aimed at a nice open field.

When I was about 100ft from the ground I saw a cyclist and heard him ring his bell. I was surprised to hear the bicycle bell and realised that I had been coming down in absolute silence. I bellowed at the cyclist, but I don't suppose he heard me. Finally, I touched down in the field and fell over. Fortunately it was a still day. My parachute just floated down and stayed down without dragging me along, as they sometimes do.

I had a piece of good news almost immediately. One of the people who came along and who had watched the combat said they had seen the Messerschmitt 110 dive straight into the sea, so it hadn't been such a bad day after all.

7 BATTLE OF BRITAIN FIGHTER ACES

ACE IN A DAY: SERGEANT RONALD HAMLYN

During the Battle of Britain, Sergeant Ronald Hamlyn was the first RAF pilot to become an 'ace' in a single day by destroying five enemy aircraft in three sorties on 24 August 1940. Flying Spitfire I R6891 'RW-Q' of No. 610 Squadron from RAF Hawkinge, having positioned from Biggin Hill in the early morning, he shot down a Junkers Ju88 on a bombing raid at 12,000ft and a Messerschmitt Bf109 off the Kent coast on his first seventy-minute sortie of the day. He took off again at 11.35 a.m. for a patrol near Dover and chased another Bf109 across the English Channel before shooting it down over Calais. Hamlyn returned for a quick lunch shortly after 1 p.m. and was soon airborne again for a third successful sortie, in which he shot down two more Bf109s

Then Sergeant Ronald Hamlyn, who was the first RAF pilot to become an 'ace' in a single day on 24 August 1940.

21 AUGUST
A Do17Z brought down at Burnham Market was the first kill by a Castle Bromwich-built Spitfire. Three Mk IIs of No. 611 Squadron were involved.

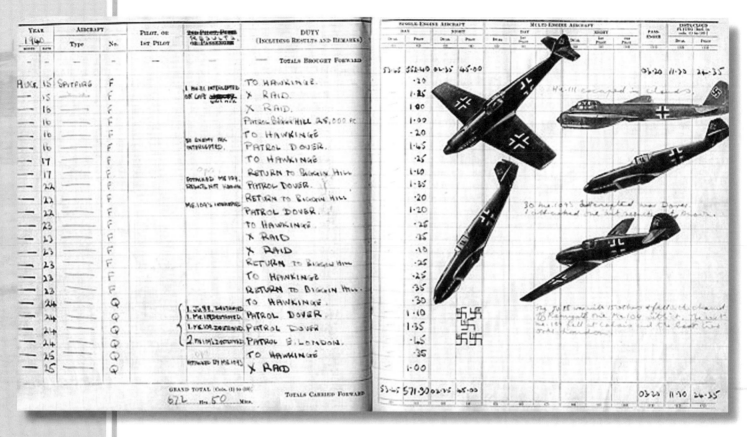

Ronald Hamlyn's illustrated page in his pilot logbook for 15–25 August.

22 AUGUST

120 Luftwaffe bomber sorties were flown against southern airfields and a night raid on the Bristol Aeroplane Company works at Filton took place. Bombs were also dropped on Edmonton and Willesden Green, Middlesex.

off the Isle of Sheppey. His three separate flights lasted just three and a half hours. He wrote in his logbook next to images of a Ju88 and Bf109s: 'The Ju88 was with 15 others and fell in the Channel off Ramsgate one Me109 with it. The next Me109 fell at Calais and the last two over London.'

Ronald Hamlyn was from Harrogate, North Yorkshire, and joined the RAF in 1936 at the age of 22. After training he was posted in October 1939 to No. 72 Squadron at RAF Drem in Scotland, flying Spitfire Is. On 2 June 1940 the squadron was sent to RAF Gravesend, Kent, and he took part in air patrols over the beaches of Dunkirk during the evacuation of Allied troops. He then joined No. 610 Squadron when it moved from Gravesend to Biggin Hill a month later. Ronald Hamlyn had destroyed two Luftwaffe aircraft prior to 24 August and brought down four more Bf109s before the end of August, bringing his total for the Battle of Britain to eleven.

Ronald Hamlyn was awarded the Distinguished Flying Medal on 13 September 1940 and the Air Force Cross (AFC) on 1 January 1943. He retired from the RAF as a wing commander in 1957 and died on 7 May 1991, aged 77.

CZECH ACE WITH A POLISH SQUADRON:
SERGEANT JOSEF FRANTIŠEK

Flying a Hurricane with No. 303 Squadron, which was formed with mainly Polish personnel, Sergeant Josef František was one of the highest-scoring RAF pilots in the Battle of Britain with seventeen 'kills' in just twenty-eight days. Born in Czechoslovakia, František learnt to fly with the Czechoslovak Air Force. After his country was taken by Germany in 1939 he fled to Poland, where he became an instructor in the Polish Air Force. He escaped from Poland and reached France, via Romania where he remained with the Polish Air Force, which was part of the French Armée de l'Air. On 18 June 1940,

Czech 'ace' Sergeant Josef František with the
mainly Polish pilots of No. 303 Squadron.

Czech pilot Sergeant Josef František was one of the RAF's top scorers in the Battle of Britain.

23 AUGUST

Night raids on the Scilly Isles, Colchester, Cardiff and Fort Dunlop, Birmingham.

after the fall of France, he managed to travel by ship from Bordeaux to England, arriving at Falmouth on 21 June. Initially sent to a Polish aviation depot in Blackpool, he joined No. 303 Squadron at RAF Northolt at the end of July. The squadron was equipped with Hurricane Is and had mainly Polish personnel. He shot down his first Luftwaffe aircraft, a Bf109E on 2 September 1940. The next day he was vectored to Dover, where he again shot down an enemy fighter. On 6 September, in heavy combat No. 303 Squadron downed five Bf109Es, but Polish losses that day were high. Three days later he was forced to land his badly damaged Hurricane. On 15 September the squadron achieved sixteen victories against the Luftwaffe, with František claiming one of them, a Bf110.

In only four weeks, from 2–30 September, his total of confirmed kills was seventeen with one probable. It is generally said that František's excellent results were due to his lack of discipline in the air. He often left the Hurricane formation and hunted for the enemy on his own. The Poles called his tactics the '*metoda* Frantiszka' (František method), while the RAF spoke of his 'lone wolf' tactics. No. 303 Squadron had shot down a confirmed total of 126 Luftwaffe aircraft in the Battle of Britain – the most successful RAF squadron at this time. Josef František was killed in unexplained circumstances on 8 October 1940 when he crashed near Ewell, Surrey, while on a routine patrol in Hurricane I R4175.

The Messerschmitt Bf110 suffered increasingly as the heavy twin-engined escort fighter was not able to dogfight effectively with Spitfires and Hurricanes.

24 AUGUST

Better weather meant the large-scale German offensive resumed with two raids on residential Dover. Manston was carpet-bombed, with smoke and dust causing bombing to drift on to Ramsgate where twenty civilians were killed, thirty fires started and 1,000 houses damaged. The town gasworks was set on fire in the heaviest raid of the battle outside of London – 500 HEs were estimated to have been dropped, some at sea. Manston was bombed and strafed again. Four raids then developed, two against RAF Hornchurch and one each on North Weald and Manston. Intelligence had suggested that London was the target, so all serviceable fighters in No. 11 Group operated. No. 12 Group's 'big wing' took too long to assemble and arrived too late. Later, fifty Junkers Ju88s delivered a four-minute 100-HE raid on Portsmouth, with many killed or injured and 700 made homeless. There were eleven incidents in inner London and six more in Greater London, the worst being at Bethnal Green rail bridge where nine people were killed and fifty-eight injured. During the day, Fighter Command flew 936 sorties – only slightly fewer than the Luftwaffe's 1,030 – and lost twenty-two fighters to the German total of twenty-five with seven damaged.

SOME OF THE DISTINGUISHED RAF FIGHTER PILOTS WHO BECAME 'ACES', DESTROYING FIVE OR MORE ENEMY AIRCRAFT, DURING THE BATTLE OF BRITAIN

Sergeant James 'Ginger' Lacey

Learning to fly in the RAF Volunteer Reserve in 1937, at the outbreak of war, 'Ginger' Lacey joined No. 501 (County of Gloucester) Squadron at Filton, flying Hurricanes. In the Battle of France he destroyed five enemy aircraft and was awarded the French Croix de Guerre. Shot down or forced to land nine times, he had many close shaves but achieved a score of twenty-three kills, fifteen of them during the Battle of Britain – including a Heinkel He111 on 13 September 1940, which he shot down after it had bombed Buckingham Palace.

'Ginger' Lacey achieved a score of twenty-three 'kills', fifteen of them during the Battle of Britain.

Squadron Leader Douglas Bader

An accomplished aerobatic pilot, a serious crash in a Bristol Bulldog in 1931 cost him both his legs. Fitted with artificial legs, Douglas rejoined the RAF as a pilot in 1939 and flew Spitfires with No. 19 Squadron and later, as a flight commander with No. 242 Squadron, Hurricanes. He achieved his first 'kill', a Messerschmitt Bf109, in June 1940 and went on to claim a further twenty-two Luftwaffe aircraft – a remarkable score considering he became a prisoner of war less than a year after the Battle of Britain. A key figure in No. 12 Group, Bader was perhaps the chief exponent of the theoretically superior but tactically inferior 'big wing' formation, advocated by the commander of No. 12 Group, Air Vice Marshal Trafford Leigh-Mallory.

Douglas Bader claimed twenty-two Luftwaffe 'kills' before he was shot down and captured.

24 AUGUST

Sergeant Ronald Hamlyn of No. 610 Squadron shot down four Bf109s and a Ju88 to become the RAF's first (and only) 'ace in a day' of the Battle of Britain.

Flight Lieutenant 'Sailor' Malan

Adolph 'Sailor' Malan, a South African, was commissioned into the RAF in 1935 from the Merchant Navy – hence the nickname. He flew with No. 74 Squadron, one of the first to receive the Spitfire in January 1939. An outstanding shot, he ordered his guns re-sighted from the usual 400 yards to a point only 250 yards distant. Appointed commanding officer of No. 74 Squadron at the height of the battle, his final tally was probably more than thirty-five, but many kills he gave to inexperienced wingmen.

Adolph 'Sailor' Malan was an outstanding combat pilot who became commanding officer of No. 74 Squadron.

Squadron Leader Peter Townsend

Commanding officer of No. 85 Squadron at RAF Martlesham Heath and Debden during the battle, he was shot down by the gunner of a Dornier Do17 on 11 July and baled out into the sea, where he spent some time before being rescued. Later wounded near Croydon, Townsend evened the score by destroying six German aircraft. He achieved further success as a night fighter pilot. He retired from the RAF as Group Captain Peter Townsend, CVO, DSO, DFC in 1956.

Squadron Leader Peter Townsend, who was Commanding Officer of No. 85 Squadron through the Battle of Britain.

Top RAF Scorers of the Battle of Britain:

Pilot Officer Eric Lock (UK):	21
Sergeant James Lacey (UK):	18
Sergeant Josef František (Czech):	17
Flight Lieutenant Archie McKellar (UK):	17

25 AUGUST

Three afternoon raids were made on Portland, Warmwell and Weymouth, Dorset.

8 AIR DEFENCE

In the mid 1930s, the importance of air superiority and how to achieve it was not fully understood by the British government. It was recognised during the First World War that speed, mobility and flexibility were the key elements of air power and that they should be coordinated to enable bombing to be more effective. However, before the introduction of radar and airborne radio communications it was impossible to coordinate these same elements for air defence. There was a widespread belief in the 1930s that air power was mainly for attack with little potential for defence – it was all about

A Gladiator biplane leading a Hurricane and Spitfire. The production of fast fighter monoplanes to replace the outdated biplanes, and in preference to bombers, was a crucial decision by the government in 1937.

25–26 AUGUST
Following the first German bombs falling on London, Bomber Command aircraft (twelve Hampdens, seventeen Wellingtons and fourteen Whitleys) made a retaliatory raid on Berlin. Comparative aircraft losses for the period 13–25 August were as follows: Luftwaffe: 281 missing, 43 write-offs, 51 major damage (total overall losses included 50 He111s, 29 Do17s, 79 Bf109s and 70 Bf110s). RAF: 185 missing, 40 write-offs, 25 major damage (total overall losses included 74 Hurricanes, 45 Spitfires).

26 AUGUST

Fighter Command airfields were again targeted. Morning activity over Kent with Folkestone bombed. Bf110-escorted Do17s dropped 160 bombs on RAF Debden. Keith Park asked Leigh-Mallory for No. 12 Group help – it arrived too late; No. 310 (Czech) Squadron engaged departing raiders. North Weald and Hornchurch raids abandoned, as the Bf109s ran short of fuel. Escorted He111s bombed Portsmouth.

No. 85 Squadron Hurricane pilots scramble at Martlesham Heath on 25 July 1940.

bombers and air assault rather than fighters and protection. In November 1932 Stanley Baldwin, then a member of the National Government, told MPs: 'I think it is well for the man in the street to realise that there is no power on earth that can protect him from being bombed. Whatever people may tell him, the bomber will always get through.' Luckily for Britain, the development of fast fighter monoplanes, the Hurricane and Spitfire in particular, convinced Chamberlain's government in 1937 that the immediate priority for air rearmament should be moved from bombers towards fighters.

In the early months of 1940, it was the German air superiority that brought about the Reich's sweeping success in Norway, Holland, Belgium and France. Three months later it was the abandonment of the German fight for air superiority over southern Britain, when the Luftwaffe switched away from 'closing down the RAF' to the blitz on major cities, that contributed significantly to its failure in the Battle of Britain.

Stepping up fighter production and training many more pilots for these Hurricanes and Spitfires enabled the RAF to focus on counter-attacking the waves of Luftwaffe bombers in the summer of 1940.

A south coast Chain Home radar station, with its 350ft-high towers with aerials strung between them.

It goes without saying that the performance of the aircraft and the skill and dedication of the pilots were essential ingredients of the victory. However, it must not be forgotten that a key to this success was the RAF's air defence control and reporting system, which used radar and radio communications.

Back in May 1935, a team of scientists under Professor Robert Watson-Watt set up a research station at Orford Ness to develop a system by which the presence, direction and range of objects could be determined by radio echoes. Radio direction finding (radar) was successfully tested at Bawdsey in 1936. On the strength of this, a chain of twenty (later twenty-seven) radar stations was built along the coast from Southampton to the Tyne. By 1939 this Chain Home had been handed over to the RAF. Alongside the Chain Home, the Post Office set up the nationwide Defence Communications Control. Permanent, duplicate and emergency telephone circuits were installed to link the radar stations to the headquarters and airfields, and a new Defence Teleprinter Network was opened in March 1939. The first of the key elements of air defence – early warning of incoming enemy aircraft – was in place.

27 AUGUST

In drizzle, lone aircraft attacked airfields. Castle Bromwich Sptifire works bombed.

In the operations room, members of the Women's Auxiliary Air Force plotted aircraft tracks by moving aircraft symbols on a huge table. From here senior officers communicated with the group operations rooms.

27/28 AUGUST
200 night raiders with bombs dropped on Greater London, Castle Bromwich and the Plymouth dock area.

Barrage balloons flown over Buckingham Palace to stop the Luftwaffe from making low-level attacks.

Air Chief Marshal Sir Hugh Dowding, appointed the First Air Officer, Commander-in-Chief of Fighter Command, in 1936, focused Britain's air defence on the use of radar. He streamlined the flow of information from the radar stations and over 1,000 Observer Corps posts via a filter room into the operations room at Fighter Command HQ at RAF Bentley Priory, Stanmore, Middlesex. Here, aircraft movements over the whole of Britain and the seas around were plotted on a huge operations table by members of the Women's Auxiliary Air Force. From this operations room, senior officers communicated with the group operations rooms: No. 10 Group – west of England and Wales; No. 11 Group – southern England; No. 12 Group – the Midlands and East Anglia; No. 13 Group – north of England, Northern Ireland, Scotland and the Orkney and Shetland Islands. They in turn

28 AUGUST

Before dawn, Gillingham was dive-bombed using incendiaries. Heavy raids by Do17s on Eastchurch and Rochford were repeated. Many Bf109s tempted RAF fighters, so Dowding ordered interceptions of bombers, not fighters. First major night raid was made on a single target – Merseyside – but bombs from 150 aircraft fell very widely.

passed it on to the appropriate sector operations rooms (SORs) within the group, to enable them in turn to control their defence assets, including squadrons, anti-aircraft guns and barrage balloons. The SORs directed the counter-attack, scrambling the fighters, positioning them in the air, updating them and helping them return, all the while passing information back to Fighter Command HQ. It was this well-planned system of early warning, communication, command and control that enabled the RAF to manage its diminishing resources to maximum effect at its most vulnerable time in the Battle of Britain.

> One reason we managed to scrape through was having radar linked to the command and control system. If we had mounted standing patrols we would never have had anything like enough aircraft, flying hours or pilots.
>
> **RAF Flight Commander**

29 AUGUST

Escorted bombers acted as Channel bait – seven Bf109s and nine RAF fighters shot down. Night incendiary raid on Merseyside warehouses and elsewhere.

"NEVER WAS SO MUCH OWED BY SO MANY TO SO FEW" *THE PRIME MINISTER*

RAF recruiting poster quoting Winston Churchill's famous words at the height of the battle.

9 WHAT IF?

By the summer of 1940, Germany's invasion plans were well advanced. Fighter Command's young pilots knew only they stood between Hitler and his dream of defeating beleaguered Britain.

Behind the scenes, British intelligence was collecting information about where precisely the Wehrmacht would choose to beach its assault barges. It transpired that Hitler's war planners were plotting to isolate England's south-western peninsula to the west of a line from Weymouth Bay to Bridgwater Bay (about 50 miles across). The plan was to land in force on the Dorset coast, then make a mechanised drive northwards through the Yeovil area.

The only German forces that landed in Britain were the crews of downed Luftwaffe fighters and bombers, who were readily captured.

30 AUGUST

Most sorties on one day to date with thirty-six aircraft shot down, twenty-six RAF fighters missing. Do17s bombed a Thames convoy. At 4 p.m. a large formation came in over Kent, potentially the most serious situation yet, headed for Langley, Oxford, Luton and several airfields. Detling was hit and Ju88s suddenly made a damaging raid on Biggin Hill. The Oxford group was forced back, but the Vauxhall factory at Luton was bombed. No warning having been given, there were huge casualties on the factory's main stairway. 1,054 sorties flown by twenty-two RAF squadrons, with some operating four times. Nine Hurricanes and six Spitfires were lost with twenty-two enemy aircraft destroyed.

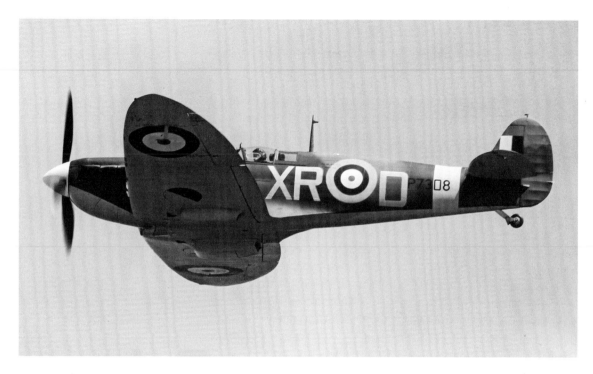

Spitfire with the markings of No. 71 Squadron, the first of the RAF's American 'Eagle' squadrons.

The ultimate aim was to occupy and use west Dorset, west Somerset, Devon and Cornwall as a base from which to launch an assault on the rest of Britain. The Nazi intention to implement this plan was evidenced by the attempt to cripple British ports by the intensive bombing of Portsmouth, Southampton, Plymouth and Bristol.

The Dorset Regiment had a battalion constituting a thin red line of defence in 1940–41 along the beaches from Weymouth eastwards through Osmington Mills to Ringstead Bay. The Dorsets also had a company inland to defend RAF Warmwell fighter station, not far from Dorchester.

It was a close-run thing, but the RAF won the battle in the skies against the Luftwaffe and the Royal Navy narrowly retained control of the English Channel. Britain's hastily manned coastal defences were not tested, although many of the men engaged in them became casualties later in the war elsewhere.

A total of 3,080 aircrew representing fourteen nations flew in the Battle of Britain; 2,543 of these were from Great Britain, with the remainder from Poland, New Zealand, Canada, Czechoslovakia, Belgium, South Africa, Australia, Free France, Eire, USA, Southern Rhodesia, Jamaica and Palestine. A total of 537 were killed, 375 of them pilots. The RAF lost 915 aircraft.

The Luftwaffe lost 1,733 aircraft, mainly bombers manned by three or four crew members.

10 OPPOSING FORCES

Britain's and Germany's air forces were organised along very different lines in 1940. The squadrons of RAF Fighter Command were virtually autonomous units, operating within a geographical area commanded by a group headquarters, so that a group could control as many squadrons as the situation demanded. At full strength, a squadron had an establishment of sixteen aircraft and up to thirty-two pilots. Normal strength was twelve aircraft in two flights of six, each of two sections of three.

In July 1940, Fighter Command faced the German threat with its squadrons controlled by four groups. In the south, No. 11 Group controlled eleven squadrons of Hurricanes, five of Spitfires and three of Blenheims. In the Midlands and East Anglia, No. 12 Group had six squadrons of Hurricanes, five of Spitfires, two of Blenheims and one of Defiants. On 18 July, No. 10 Group became operational in the south-west with four squadrons of Spitfires and four of Hurricanes. The rest of the UK – the north of England, Scotland, Northern Ireland and the Orkney and Shetland Islands – was covered by No. 13 Group with four squadrons of Hurricanes, four of Spitfires, one of Blenheims and one of Defiants. Group areas were divided into sectors, each consisting of a main airfield (sector station) and usually at least one satellite base.

There were twenty-one squadrons of Hurricane Is operational with Nos 10, 11 and 12 Groups in July 1940.

31 AUGUST

Four major onslaughts on airfields: the first on Eastchurch, Debden, and Duxford and Fowlmere; the second a heavy raid by He111s on Croydon and Biggin Hill, with Hornchurch bombed as No. 54 Squadron scrambled; the third a series of attacks on radar stations in Kent and Sussex and a small attack on Hornchurch; the fourth saw 300 bombers attacking airfields in Kent and near London. Thirty-eight German aircraft (twenty-nine fighters) were destroyed; the RAF lost twenty-five Hurricanes and nine Spitfires. Flt Lt R. Smith scored a probable, the first by a cannon-armed No. 151 Squadron Hurricane (V7360). Leeds and Merseyside were also bombed that night.

Fighter Command was supported by Coastal Command's fourteen squadrons – four with Blenheims and ten with bomber or torpedo bombers – together with a further dozen day-bomber squadrons of Bomber Command's No. 2 Group, and by a handful of Fleet Air Arm fighters and biplane torpedo bombers. All played a part in the Battle of Britain.

The Luftwaffe unit was the Gruppe, with up to five Gruppen forming a Geschwader, the largest flying unit in the Luftwaffe. Each Gruppe contained three Staffeln, and each Staffel had about twelve aircraft, with eight or nine normally operational.

Geschwadern and Gruppen carried a prefix indicating their role, for example:

- Jagd – Fighter
- Kampf – Bomber
- Stuka – Dive bomber
- Schlacht – Ground attack
- Lehr – Special test

Although a Gruppe would usually occupy one airfield and operate as a component, Staffeln were self-contained entities with their own traditions, ground crew, badges and sometimes colour schemes. Larger groupings were formed according to requirement: several Geschwadern or autonomous Gruppen formed a Fliegerkorps (air corps), while a number of Fliegerkorps formed a Luftflotte (air fleet).

Staffeln and Gruppen were numbered as part of their Geschwader, Staffeln being identified by Arabic numbers and Gruppen by Roman, so II Gruppe of Kampfsgeschwader 53, for example, was identified by the abbreviation II/KG 53. Staffeln were numbered within Gruppen:

- I Gruppe – 1-3 Staffeln
- II Gruppe – 4-6 Staffeln
- III Gruppe – 7-9 Staffeln

For example: 9/JG2 indicates 9 Staffel within III Gruppe of Jagdgeschwader 2.

At the Luftwaffe's disposal in July 1940 were three Luftflotten (air fleets). The biggest, Luftflotte 2, was based in Belgium and northern France, facing England from the east, while Luftflotte 3 was stationed in Normandy and poised to strike at the south coast. The smaller Luftflotte 5 had been based in Denmark and Norway since the spring of 1940; its targets were in Scotland and the north of England.

Dornier Do17Zs of KG77 based in northern France in August 1940.

Heinkel He111Hs returning to France after a bombing mission.

1 SEPTEMBER

Four morning raids, with the bombers surrounded by many fighters, but they mainly bombed minor airfields. Low-flying Dornier Do17s bombed Biggin Hill; its operations room was devastated. WAAFs Sgt Helen Turner and Cpl Elspeth Henderson were both awarded the Military Medal for keeping at their posts. Hawkinge and Lympne were strafed.

2 SEPTEMBER

Four major early morning attacks were made on Rochford, North Weald, Biggin Hill and Gravesend. Low-flying Do17s again bombed Biggin Hill and there was a large-scale noon bombing of Maidstone. A fierce battle in the late afternoon involved ninety RAF fighters versus 100 Luftwaffe. Seven airfields were attacked, including Eastchurch. The RAF lost twenty-two fighters with nine badly damaged, and the Luftwaffe lost twenty-four shot down and ten damaged.

A flight of No. 601 Squadron Hurricane Is based at Tangmere in the summer of 1940.

THE LINE-UP ON 10 AUGUST 1940

RAF Fighter Command

Commanded by Air Chief Marshal Sir Hugh Dowding from his headquarters at RAF Bentley Priory, RAF Fighter Command had twenty-six squadrons of Hurricanes, nineteen squadrons of Spitfires and nine squadrons of Blenheim/Defiant night fighters at his disposal.

The aircraft were divided amongst the four groups, with the total number of each type of aircraft allocated and the numbers (in brackets) actually operational on 10 August 1940, as follows:

No. 10 Group: Spitfires 63 (42); Hurricanes 50 (37); Blenheims 16 (11).
No. 11 Group: Spitfires 96 (70); Hurricanes 216 (165); Blenheims 36 (20).
No. 12 Group: Spitfires 61 (41); Hurricanes 51 (37); Blenheims 26 (17); Defiants 16 (12).
No. 13 Group: Spitfires 75 (55); Hurricanes 149 (111); Blenheims 15 (10); Defiants 12 (8);
    Gladiators 14 (8); Fulmars 12 (8).

No. 610 (County of Chester) Squadron, Auxiliary Air Force, Spitfire Ias on patrol over Kent while operating from Biggin Hill in August 1940.

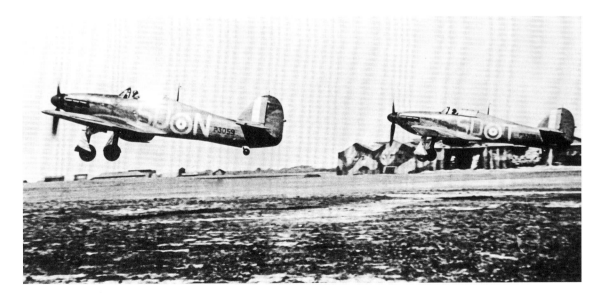

Two Hurricane Is of No. 501 (County of Gloucester) Squadron, Auxiliary Air Force, scramble from Hawkinge on 15 August 1940.

3 SEPTEMBER

Heavy attacks on RAF airfields continued, mainly concentrated on North Weald and Debden. An equal number of RAF fighters and Luftwaffe aircraft – sixteen each – were shot down. Eight of the RAF pilots were saved.

A Ju87 Stuka of I/StG 1 (1 Staffeln within I Gruppe).

4 SEPTEMBER

The Vickers factory at Weybridge was attacked and a succession of airfield raids was made by 300 German bombers. The Luftwaffe was now turning its attention to aircraft manufacturing and aero-engine works, in an abortive attempt to halt the flow of fighters to the RAF.

The Luftwaffe

Commanded by Reichsmarschall Hermann Göring, the Luftwaffe had five Luftflotten (air forces), each having a designated geographical area of responsibility. Three of these forces were principally engaged in the Battle of Britain: Luftflotte II, HQ Brussels (northern France, Belgium and the Netherlands); Luftflotte III, HQ Paris (north-west France); and Luftflotte V, HQ Stavanger, Norway (Scandinavia).

These Luftflotten had the following aircraft allocated, with the figure in brackets showing the number actually operational on 10 August:

Luftflotten II & III: Heinkel He111, Junkers Ju88, Dornier Do17 bombers 1,233 (875); Ju87 dive-bombers 406 (316); Messerschmitt Bf109 fighters 813 (702); Messerschmitt Bf110 fighter-bombers 282 (227); other reconnaissance aircraft 65 (46).

Luftflotte V: Heinkel He111, Junkers Ju88, Dornier Do17 bombers 138 (123); Messerschmitt Bf110 fighter-bombers 37 (34); other reconnaissance aircraft 48 (33).

Despite greater speed than the He111 and Do17, the Junkers Ju88 bomber proved vulnerable to the RAF's fighters at medium level.

The Luftwaffe had over 700 Bf109Es operational in France, Belgium and the Netherlands in July 1940.

Messerschmitt Bf110Cs of II Gruppe of ZG 26, known as the Haifischgruppe (shark wing), dispersed at an airfield in northern France in the summer of 1940.

5 SEPTEMBER

Airfields attacked again with Croydon, Biggin Hill, Detling, Eastchurch, North Weald and Lympne the main targets. Fourteen RAF squadrons joined the fight and lost twenty-three aircraft – Spitfires and Hurricanes – against twenty Luftwaffe losses. That night Liverpool, Manchester, London and numerous other towns were raided.

REMEMBERING THE BATTLE

At the 75th anniversary of the Battle of Britain, there are four airworthy fighters in the UK that actually took part in the Battle. There is one RAF Spitfire (Mk IIA P7350) and a Hurricane (Mk I R4118), together with a solitary Luftwaffe Messerschmitt BF109E (w.nr 3579 'White 14'). In addition, a Bristol Blenheim (Mk IF L6739) night-fighter has been reconstructed from the airframe of Blenheim IV/Bolingbroke (RCAF 10201/G-BPIV).

Photographed in 2010, P7350 is painted in No. 616 Squadron colours.

BBMF Spitfire IIA P7350 wearing No. 603 Squadron markings in 2004.

SPITFIRE IIA P7350

The Battle of Britain Memorial Flight's P7350 is the only airworthy Spitfire to have taken part in the Battle of Britain. Built at Castle Bromwich it entered service in August 1940, and flew with No. 266 (Rhodesia) Squadron coded UO-T and No. 603 (City of Edinburgh) Squadron, believed coded XT-L, during the Battle of Britain. In the latter squadron's service, it was damaged in combat with Luftwaffe Bf109s and made a forced landing near Hastings on 25 October 1940. Repaired, it was back in action the following year with No. 616 Squadron at Tangmere. P7350 was retired in July 1944 and stored until sold for scrap in 1947. The owner presented it back to RAF Colerne. In 1967 it was restored to flying condition for the film *Battle of Britain*, after which it was allocated to the Battle of Britain Memorial Flight.

HURRICANE I R4118

Peter Vacher's R4118 is the only flying example of a Hurricane I that was involved in the Battle of Britain. Gloster-built, it was delivered to No. 605 Squadron on 17 August 1940 and coded UP-W. R4118 subsequently made forty-nine combat sorties during which pilots claimed five enemy 'kills' including one confirmed Ju88 and another probable, with Wing Commander Bob Foster flying it on both occasions. During the forty-ninth flight on 22 October 1940, R4118 received battle damage which put it out of action until early 1941. It next flew with No. 111 Squadron and several operational training units before being exported to India in 1943 for further training use. Nearly sixty years later Peter Vacher recovered it to the UK and Hawker Restorations commenced an intense restoration programme. Battle of Britain veteran R4118 was airborne again on 23 December 2004.

Peter Vacher's immaculate Hurricane I R4118 carries the code UP-W, as it did when it was first delivered to No. 605 Squadron on 17 August 1940.

MESSERSCHMITT BF109E-4 W.NR 3579 'WHITE 14'

Bf109E w.nr 3579 was built by Arado and taken on charge by the Luftwaffe in November 1939. By April 1940 it was painted as 'White 14' and flying with 1.(Jagd)/LG2 at Westerland. In July 1940 LG2 moved to Calais-Marck airfield. Cadet Officer Hans-Joachem Marseille (who went on to become a top Luftwaffe ace) claimed a Spitfire over Kent on 2 September while flying 'White 14' but later the same day he was damaged by a No. 74 Squadron Spitfire and crash-landed near Calais-Marck, resulting in 50 per cent damage to the aircraft. It was rebuilt as a Bf109E-7 and joined 4/JG5 as 'White 7' on the Eastern Front and again suffered a crash-landing in a marsh at Pya Ozero, northern Russia, on 2 August 1942. No. 3579 was recovered from Russia in 1991 and rebuilt, flying again as 'White 14' at Chino, CA on 29 September 1999. It was based in Canada from mid 2004 until sold to its present UK owner in 2014.

Rebuilt Messerschmitt Bf109E w.nr 3579 flies as Hans-Joachem Marseille's 'White 14'.

BLENHEIM IF L6739

Blenheim IF L6739 was a participant in the Battle of Britain and its original nose section now features within the world's only airworthy Blenheim variant. Avro-built, L6739 was delivered to No. 23 Squadron at RAF Wittering on 2 September 1939. After moving with the squadron to RAF Collyweston on 31 May 1940, it made a forced landing on 13 August and was damaged. At the end of that year L6739 was struck off charge and, after the war, broken up at Filton. Its nose section was acquired by a Bristol Aeroplane Company employee and, using parts of an Austin 7, made into an unusual electric car. Donated to the restoration of crashed Blenheim IV/Bolingbroke 10201 G-BPIV, L6739's reconstructed nose was first joined to the fuselage in May 2008. On 20 November 2014, the composite airframe made its first post-restoration flight at Duxford, painted with L6739's original No. 23 Squadron scheme, including the code YP-Q.

Duxford-based Blenheim IF L6739 is painted with its original No. 23 Squadron code from 1940.

The towering statue of Sir Keith Park, and boards displaying RAF/Luftwaffe unit badges, in the Battle of Britain Hall at the RAF Museum.

Supermarine Spitfire I X4590 was built at Southampton in 1940 and delivered to the RAF in September 1940, moving to No. 609 Squadron at Middle Wallop coded PR-F on 8 October 1940. It was flown operationally two days later.

BATTLE OF BRITAIN HALL AT THE RAF MUSEUM

The RAF Museum's Battle of Britain Hall tells the story of the world's first decisive air battle, when the RAF stood alone against the might of the German Luftwaffe in 1940.

Refurbished in 2010, the aircraft collection contains the most comprehensive selection of aircraft from both sides that fought in the Battle of Britain. Alongside these aeroplanes the interactive displays provide an insight into the minds and actions of those who experienced the Battle at first hand.

Special features introduced into the Battle of Britain Hall include the presentation of previously unseen footage from the 1969 film *Battle of Britain*, new panels giving added insight into history, key personalities and Battle of Britain operations, a 15m-high statue honouring Sir Keith Park, whose command of RAF No. 11 Group Fighter Command was integral to the RAF's success in the battle; 'Our Finest Hour', the museum's sound and light show, which explains the battle; and a permanent exhibition, 'Art of the Battle of Britain', located on the mezzanine level.

Hawker Hurricane I P2617 was built by Gloster Aircraft in 1939 and delivered to the RAF on 19 January 1940. It was flown operationally by No. 607 Squadron in France from 14 April until 20 May 1940 and based at Croydon until 26 October when it moved to Prestwick to join No. 401 Squadron. It made a wheels-up landing on 20 November 1940.

The only surviving complete Boulton Paul Defiant I, N1671, was taken on RAF charge in August 1940 and operated by No. 307 (Polish) Squadron from September 1940, being operational from December 1940 after working up and training. Its last operational use was with No. 285 (Anti-Aircraft Co-Operation) Squadron from June 1942.

Messerschmitt Bf109E-4/B w.nr 4101 was completed by Erla Maschinenwerk at Leipzig in 1940 and delivered to JG51 at Pihen in northern France on 5 September. It was modified to carry a 250kg bomb under the fuselage and passed to 2/JG51 at Wissant near Calais. On 27 November it was damaged by a Spitfire of No. 66 Squadron and crash-landed in Kent.

Heinkel He111 H-20/R1 w.nr 701152 was built in 1944 to carry sixteen paratroops and three crew. Its Luftwaffe service before the German surrender in May 1945 is not known.

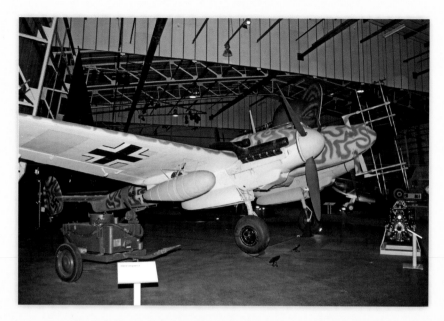

Messerschmitt Bf110-4/R6 w.nr 730301 is believed to have been manufactured in 1944 as a night fighter. It was operational with 1/NJG3 (1st Staffel of Nachtjagdgeschwader 3) at Karup, Denmark, in 1945 coded D5+RL.

Junkers Ju87G-2 w.nr 494083 was originally built as Ju87D-5 w.nr 2883 and subsequently converted to a Ju87G-2 for ground attack duties. It was captured near the Russian border in May 1945.

11 RAF FIGHTERS

SUPERMARINE SPITFIRE

The progressive thinking of aircraft designer R.J. Mitchell and his team at Supermarine produced the legendary Spitfire. Through work for the RAF's High Speed Flight and its Schneider Trophy contenders, that culminated in outright victory for Britain in 1931, the company knew more than anyone about streamlining, structural stressing, control surface flutter and other special problems associated with high-speed flight. The Spitfire was the outcome of a process of development and refinement of a single-seat fighter design which Mitchell originally conceived as a private venture

A Rolls-Royce Merlin III engine that powered the Spitfire, Hurricane and Defiant fighters.

R.J. Mitchell (left) with Henry Royce.

because he was dissatisfied with a Rolls-Royce Goshawk-powered fighter he had proposed to a rigid 1930 Air Ministry specification. Mitchell decided that the firm's experience with racing aircraft could be applied to the design of land-based fighters. The result was an all-metal design (apart from control surfaces) with a distinctive elliptical wing shape and an eight-machine-gun armament. However, it was the emergence of the Rolls-Royce PV.12 engine – later named Merlin – that was to be the most important catalyst in Spitfire development. The Spitfire was of such advanced conception that the Official Specification F.37/34 had to be virtually 'written round it' when the Air Ministry contract was produced in the winter of 1934–35.

The prototype, with the serial K5054, first flew at Eastleigh, near Southampton, on 5 March 1936, with Capt. J. 'Mutt' Summers, the Vickers (Aviation) Group's chief test pilot, at the controls. Its Merlin engine with a fixed-pitch two-bladed wooden propeller gave it a maximum speed of 342mph (542.2km/h). After this successful first flight an order for 310 aircraft was placed and the name Spitfire chosen: 'Just the sort of bloody silly name they would choose', commented Mitchell. Unfortunately he never heard more than a tiny fraction of the praise that was lavished on the Spitfire, since he died of cancer in June 1937 at the tragically early age of 42.

6 SEPTEMBER
While the Luftwaffe suffered its biggest single day's loss (thirty-three destroyed) Fighter Command was weakening, having lost 119 aircraft since 1 September, with many experienced pilots, including five squadron leaders and eight flight commanders, killed since 26 August.

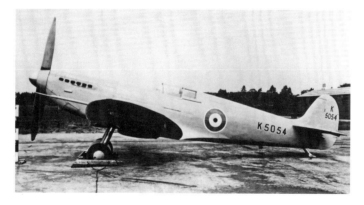

The prototype Spitfire K5054 at Eastleigh Airport, Southampton, in March 1936.

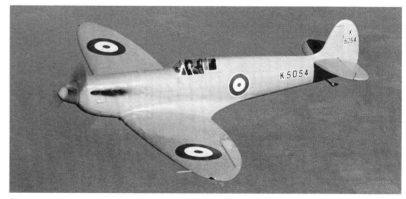

Capt. J. 'Mutt' Summers, the Vickers (Aviation) group's chief test pilot, first flew the Spitfire prototype on 5 March 1936.

The government's order for Spitfires was increased to 510 in 1937, the year that production commenced. The first of 1,583 Supermarine Spitfire Is with a 1,030hp Rolls-Royce Merlin II driving a fixed-pitch wooden propeller entered service with the RAF in August 1938, in the hands of No. 19 Squadron at RAF Duxford. Early improvements soon available included two-position controllable pitch propellers and an engine-driven hydraulic pump. Production Spitfires had a more 'humpy' engine cowling than the sleek prototype. New ejector exhausts were fitted, which provided some extra thrust to offset some of the humps. The first aircraft had a flush cockpit, but this was soon bulged on top as it restricted the height of the pilot that could be accommodated. The canopy slid to the rear and a hinged panel on the port side of the fuselage-assisted entry and exit. The seat and rudder pedals were adjustable.

The first production Spitfire I K9787 flying in 1938.

Compact cockpit of the Spitfire I.

7 SEPTEMBER

The Battle of Britain entered a new phase with the opening of the 'blitz on London'. Luftwaffe bombing switched to the capital, thereby reducing the pressure on fighter airfields. Around 4.30 p.m., 360 raiders reached Deal, flew on to the Thames Estuary and headed for London, bombing major installations as they proceeded. Around Woolwich Arsenal, thirty fires were started. The sixteen RAF fighter squadrons scrambled were unable to halt the armada. At 5.50 p.m. bombs began raining down on London's dockland. Bermondsey became a conflagration and Silvertown was engulfed by fire. Long feared, the attempted destruction of London had begun. Luftflotte III brutally increased the pain of the London blitz with a ten-hour night onslaught ending at 4.30 a.m. London was burning and invasion seemed imminent, so Bomber Command began an intensive bombing of Channel ports from Flushing westwards.

8 SEPTEMBER

Two daylight operations over Kent preceded very widespread, lengthy night bombing of London. South London came under daylight bombardment the following morning.

At the outbreak of the Second World War on 3 September 1939, Spitfires equipped seven RAF squadrons (Nos 19, 41, 54, 65, 66, 72 and 74) and two Royal Auxiliary Air Force squadrons (Nos 602 and 611). When the Mk I entered service it had a maximum diving speed of 450mph and its initial rate of climb was 2,500ft per minute. Its top speed (367mph) was marginally higher than the Messerschmitt Bf109E, its principal opponent at the time. One significant change with the production Spitfire I was the fitting of external armour-glass windscreens, provided at the insistence of Fighter Command's Commander-in-Chief, Air Chief Marshal Sir Hugh Dowding, who pointed out that if Chicago gangsters could ride behind bulletproof glass he saw no reason why his pilots should not.

The Mk I was followed by the Spitfire II, which was similar except that it was fitted with a 1,175hp Merlin XII engine with a Rotol constant-speed, three-bladed propeller, and had 73lb of armour plate. The Merlin XII had a Coffman cartridge starter, but was otherwise a single-speed supercharged engine like the Merlin II. The first Spitfire IIs were delivered to No. 611 Squadron in August 1940.

Spitfire I X4382 of No. 602 (City of Glasgow) Squadron at RAF Westhampnett in September 1940.

A Spitfire IIA in No. 19 Squadron markings. The improved Mk IIAs replaced the Mk Is with the squadron in September 1940.

With the start of the Battle of Britain in 1940, it was soon realised that the two-position propellers fitted to the Spitfire were inadequate for climb and ceiling, although they fulfilled their original purpose of improving take-off performance. Subsequently either de Havilland or Rotol constant-speed, variable-pitch propellers were fitted, both on delivery and by modification in the field. The resulting improvement in climb and ceiling did much to help combat the Luftwaffe at this difficult time. Also during the Battle of Britain it was realised that eight machine guns alone were barely adequate, so a variant of the Mk II was produced with four improved 0.303mm Browning machine guns, with the rate of fire increased from 1,100 to 1,200 rounds per minute, and two 20mm cannon. The new type was known as the Spitfire IIb, while the original eight-machine-gun version was redesignated Spitfire IIa. The early cannon proved troublesome in initial trials when the feed and ejector mechanism jammed, and it was not until late 1940 that cannon-armed Spitfires performed satisfactorily in service. A total of 1,567 Spitfire I/Ias and 921 Spitfire II/IIa/IIbs were built.

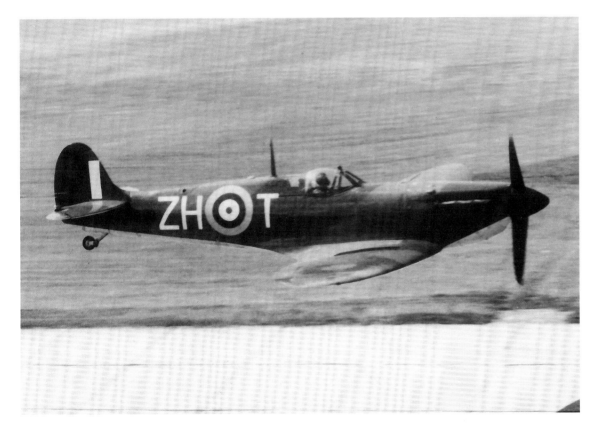

No. 266 Squadron first received Spitfire IIas at Wittering in September 1940. This image shows shows a Mk IIa with the No. 266 Squadron code letters.

9 SEPTEMBER

Raids did not commence until the evening, but Fighter Command interceptions were so successful that most formations were broken up before reaching their targets. Twenty-eight German aircraft were lost and nineteen RAF fighters from which six pilots were saved.

HAWKER HURRICANE

The Hawker Hurricane began its evolution in 1933, when Sydney Camm, the then chief designer of Hawker Aircraft Limited, looked at the idea of a high-performance monoplane interceptor to replace the RAF's Fury biplane. He saw the only way forward to increase fighter performance was to move from the established biplane (two-wing) to a monoplane (single-wing) configuration. Broadly resembling the Fury, his design featured a new metal stressed-skin wing with flaps, self-sealing fuel tanks, an inwards retracting undercarriage with wide-spaced legs and wheels to give good stability on the ground, a fully enclosed cockpit with armour plating and bulletproof windscreen, with the canopy mounted relatively high to give good visibility for the pilot. One of the new Rolls-Royce PV.12 engines (later named Merlin) providing 1,030hp (768kW) was chosen to power the fighter. It was built to meet Air Ministry Specification F.36/34, the prototype (K5083) making its first flight on 6 November 1935, in the hands of chief test pilot Group Captain P.W.S. 'George' Bulman. On landing after the maiden flight, Bulman told Camm: 'It is a piece of cake; I could even teach you to fly her in half an hour.'

10 SEPTEMBER

Coastal towns and Channel convoys were bombed before 300 aircraft again attacked south London, facing twenty-four RAF fighter squadrons. The early September respite, the switch to bombing London, the failure to destroy fighter production or enough of Fighter Command's airfields and active fighters, coupled with anti-aircraft defences, resulted in a resurgence of British defences, backed to the north by extensive reserves.

K5083, the prototype Hurricane, was airborne for the first time on 6 November 1935. On landing, chief test pilot Group Captain 'George' Bulman told chief designer Sydney Camm: 'It is a piece of cake; I could even teach you to fly her in half an hour.'

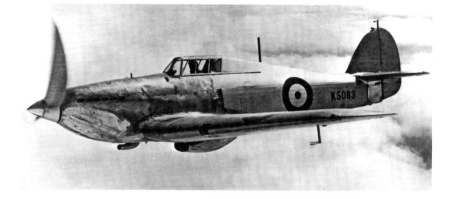

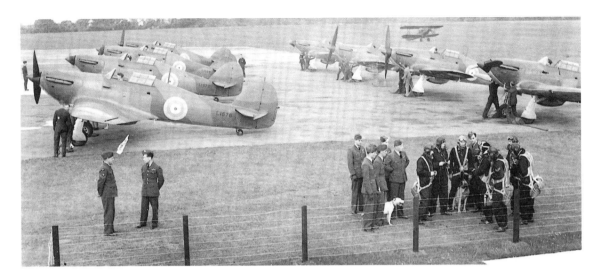

Hurricane Is of No. 111 Squadron at Northolt early in 1938 for a press day.

Hurricanes of No. 87 Squadron (photo) were sent to France with the British Expeditionary Force at the outbreak of the Second World War.

Put into production three months before the official order for 600 aircraft was placed on 20 July 1936, the first Hurricane I flew on 12 October 1937. Initially driving a fixed-pitch two-blade wooden propeller, it had a maximum speed of 318mph reached at 16,250ft. The Hurricane's armament comprised four pairs of machine guns carried in the wings and firing outside of the propeller arc. The American Colt Browning machine gun was chosen and adapted to take the existing rifle-calibre bullet of 0.303in. A total of 300 rounds of ammunition per gun was carried, giving just fourteen seconds of continuous fire.

Only five RAF squadrons were equipped with Hurricanes by early 1938. The first of these, No. 111 Squadron at RAF Northolt, received its aircraft in January that year. By the end of 1938, the German air force's front-line strength was over 3,000 against the RAF's total of 2,000. The uprated Merlin III that began flight testing in January 1939 had a de Havilland (licence-built Hamilton

11 SEPTEMBER
Small daytime raids took place on CW11 aircraft works, Portsmouth, Tangmere and Poling radar station. Cunliffe-Owen aircraft works at Southampton was dive-bombed by Bf110s. London once again received a nine-hour night assault.

12 SEPTEMBER

Numerous single raiders were active, one bombing Harrogate, Yorkshire, home of the Ministry of Aircraft Production. Widespread night raids with 168 people killed and 689 wounded in the twenty-four hours to 6 a.m. on the 13th.

Standard) or Rotol constant-speed propeller and ejector exhausts quickly becoming standard on production aircraft. A reflector gunsight was another important addition soon after the Hurricane had its first combat experience.

At the outbreak of the war, Hurricanes were chosen to accompany the RAF bomber squadrons sent to France with the British Expeditionary Force where they received their 'baptism of fire'. They equipped Nos 1 and 73 Squadrons of the Advanced Air Striking Force and Nos 85 and 87 Squadrons of the Air Component. The first enemy aircraft shot down by RAF pilots, a Dornier Do17, was destroyed by Hurricane L1842 of No. 1 Squadron, on 30 October 1939.

When the Battle of France began in May 1940, German bombers attacked twenty-one Allied airfields. No. 8 Squadron with its Hurricanes put up fierce resistance. In one day ninety Luftwaffe aircraft were shot down for the loss of twenty RAF fighters. A further thirty-two Hurricanes were

King George VI taking a close look at a newly delivered Hurricane I in May 1938.

sent to France, but Air Chief Marshal Sir Hugh Dowding, Commander-in-Chief of Fighter Command, resisted sending more. A total of 200 Hurricanes were lost in France (about seventy-five to enemy action) by the end of May. Unfortunately many had to be destroyed on the ground to save them falling into German hands during the evacuation.

On 3 June 1940, at the thick of the Battle for Dunkirk, Hurricanes were sent from England to defend the British Expeditionary Force and cover the evacuation from the beaches. Some sixteen Hurricane squadrons were in action at any one time. A total of thirty-two fighter squadrons, twenty-five of which were equipped with Hurricanes, saw combat over the Channel Ports, from which 477 aircraft were lost, including 300 Hurricanes. After Dunkirk there were only 367 Hurricanes and Spitfires remaining for the defence of Britain.

Although it had been at the forefront of the air war over France, the Hurricane really won its spurs during the Battle of Britain. Fighter Command's average Hurricane strength between 10 July and 31 October 1940 was 1,326, compared with 957 Spitfires, making it the RAF's principal fighter. There were thirty-two Hurricane squadrons in Fighter Command and nineteen equipped with Spitfires.

By the end of the Battle of Britain the Hurricane I had accounted for more enemy aircraft than had any other Allied type; while 695 Hurricanes had been lost, over 1,500 Luftwaffe aircraft had been shot down, two thirds by Hurricanes. This achievement confirmed that Camm's design had qualities which compensated for its lack of performance compared with the German Bf109.

BRISTOL BLENHEIM I

In 1934 Viscount Rothermere instructed the Bristol Aeroplane Company to build him a passenger aircraft that would be 'the best in the world'. Within a year *Britain First* was delivered, and he immediately donated it to the RAF. This Bristol Type 142 became the prototype for the Blenheim powered by two 840hp (627kW) Bristol Mercury VIII engines, which was faster than most fighters then in service.

The first Bristol 142M Blenheim light bomber.

13 SEPTEMBER
Buckingham Palace was bombed during eight hours of Luftwaffe attacks.

No. 114 Squadron received its first Blenheim I
K7040 in March 1937 at Wyton.

Blenheims on the production line at Filton.

14 SEPTEMBER

Fighter-bomber raids
on London, after which
the Bf109s and Bf110s
without their bombs
became agile fighters,
but with very limited
endurance.

Although the Type 142M Blenheim was a very advanced light bomber for the mid 1930s and comparable with other new aircraft being developed in Germany and elsewhere, by the outbreak of the Second World War it was being overtaken. In the autumn of 1939, seven home-based fighter squadrons were equipped with Blenheim IF fighters that had a ventral pack housing four Browning 0.303 in machine guns fitted to augment the standard single forward-firing machine gun.

In the Battle of France in May 1940, these cumbersome Blenheim day fighters with their slow turning rate suffered crippling losses, being no match for agile Luftwaffe fighters. Some 200 were converted to serve as night fighters, pioneering the newly conceived technique of AI (Airborne

Interception) radar. No. 600 Squadron at RAF Manston was the first to have its aircraft equipped with the AI Mk III radar. The first ever AI success against an enemy aircraft by a night fighter was achieved by a Blenheim IF from the Fighter Command Fighter Interception Unit at Ford, Sussex on the night of 2–3 July 1940. They continued with moderate success as night fighters until mid 1941, by which time most had been replaced by Bristol Beaufighter IFs.

BOULTON PAUL DEFIANT I

First flown on 11 August 1937, powered by a 1,030hp (768kW) Rolls-Royce Merlin engine, the Boulton Paul Defiant was introduced to replace the Hawker Demon in Fighter Command. The two-crew aircraft had a large, heavy, four-gun turret mounted within the fuselage behind the pilot. The weight and drag of the turret restricted the speed, rate of climb and manoeuvrability of the newcomer.

Delivery of the first Defiant I day fighters to No. 264 Squadron began in December 1939 and the squadron saw its first action on 12 May 1940 over Dunkirk's beaches. Against bombers the Defiant's turret armament was very effective at first, and by operating mixed formations of Defiants and Hurricanes the RAF could make use of the superficial resemblance between the two types to confuse the German fighters. This tactical surprise was only brief. When the Messerschmitts caught Defiants on their own, they found they could attack head-on or from below with immunity and inflict heavy casualties. As a consequence the Defiant was withdrawn from daylight operations by August 1940 and modified for the night fighter role.

Fitted with the Airborne Interception (AI) Mk IV radar, the Defiant NFIA was more successful. A night fighter pilot later said, 'During the night blitz in 1940–41 the Defiant shot down more enemy aircraft than any other type, and had more kills per interception and more interceptions per 100 sorties … Curiously, nothing was done to develop either the NF Defiant itself or the valuable attribute of upward-firing armament.' At its peak as a night fighter the Defiant saw service with thirteen RAF squadrons but by mid 1942 had been relegated to target-tug duties.

Defiant I day fighters were initially flown by No. 264 Squadron from Duxford. The middle of these three aircraft, N1535 'PS-A', was shot down on 24 August 1940 along with two other Defiants. As a result the squadron switched to night fighting.

15 SEPTEMBER

This date has since been recognised as Battle of Britain Day. There was good weather, and the first massive daylight bombing of London since 7 September started. The first wave, Do17s of KG 3, faced head-on attacks by Douglas Bader's Hurricanes. They penetrated the Luftwaffe fighter screen and forced the bombers to turn back. The next inflow met 170 fighters and Mallory's No. 12 Group Wing. The bombers fled, unloading their bombs widely over south-east London. During the day the Luftwaffe flew over 1,000 sorties and the RAF fighters 705. Fighter Command was still as strong as in mid August; the failure to destroy it – and the Royal Navy – made a successful German invasion impossible. The BBC midnight news claimed that 188 German aircraft were shot down. Confusion had inflated the probable loss of some fifty aircraft (including eleven He111s, two Ju88s and nineteen Bf109s). RAF fighter losses totalled twenty-eight, including twenty Hurricanes. What made 15 September 1940 Battle of Britain Day was the clear and repeated routing of the enemy despite the onslaught inflicted for many weeks upon the RAF. It was a significant victory, which brought about a major boost to the nation's morale.

12 LUFTWAFFE FIGHTERS AND BOMBERS

MESSERSCHMITT Bf109

The Messerschmitt Bf109 was the Luftwaffe's principal fighter throughout the Second World War and is recognised as one of the world's great fighter aircraft. It was built in greater number (30,500) than any other warplane apart from the Soviet Il-2. Designed by Willy Messerschmitt at Bayerische Flugzeugwerke (hence the Bf prefix) and first flown in 1935, the Bf109 entered service just in time to be used in the Spanish Civil War. Initially powered by a 1,100hp (821kW) Daimler-Benz DB601A 12-cylinder, inverted-V, liquid-cooled engine, the Bf109E 'Emil' appeared in 1938 and the Luftwaffe had about 1,000 in service at the outbreak of the Second World War.

The 'Emil' saw its first action against the RAF on 18 December 1939 when an unescorted Wellington was shot down over Wilhelmshaven. The Bf109 was at the forefront throughout 1940 in all German campaigns, including the Battle of Britain. It proved superior to the Hurricane I and Spitfire I in respect of its more effective cannon armament and the fuel injection system of its Daimler-Benz engine which kept the engine running at full power when inverted or in high-G turns. However it did have some significant drawbacks – it had an inferior turn performance to those of the RAF's fighter pair, restricted

This Bf109E-4 was flown by 1.(Jagd)/LG2 from Calais until it made a crash-landing on 2 September 1940.

Bf109E-3 'White 1' of JG76 made a forced landing in France on 22 November 1939. After evaluation by the French it was handed over to the RAF in May 1940 and given the serial AE479 before being exhaustively tested at RAE Farnborough and the Air Fighting Development Unit at Northolt.

vision from the cockpit, and bad landing characteristics, while its relatively short range meant that it had insufficient fuel to stay and fight for more than a few minutes over England. The capabilities of the 'Emil' were also too often tied to close escort of bomber formations. A total of 610 Bf109s were lost during the Battle of Britain.

It remained the backbone of the Luftwaffe fighter arm until the end of the war, proving adaptable enough to accept new engines and weapons with minimum modifications. Post-war, fitted with Rolls-Royce Merlin engines, Bf109s were built under licence in Spain as HA-1112 Buchóns.

MESSERSCHMITT Bf110

The twin-engined, two-crew Messerschmitt Bf110, first flown in 1936, was designed as a long-range, heavily armed escort fighter and fighter-bomber and was powered by two 1,100hp (821kW) Daimler-Benz DB601A 12-cylinder engines. While the two 20mm MG FF cannon and four 7.92mm MG17 machine guns in its nose and the 7.92mm MG15 machine gun on a flexible mount in the rear of the cockpit gave it formidable firepower, its heavy weight restricted its manoeuvrability. Initially the Bf110 was virtually immune to attacks from fighter aircraft while above 22,000ft, but with the Luftwaffe lacking air superiority in the Battle of Britain the use of the Bf110 as an escort

These Messerschmitt Bf110 Zerstörers were virtually immune to the RAF's fighters above 22,000ft escorting bombers but were no match for their opponents at lower levels.

17 SEPTEMBER

Hitler ordered that Operation *Sea Lion*, the planned invasion of southern England, be postponed until further notice.

fighter was disastrous. Although it could out-climb the Spitfire I it was too vulnerable in a dogfight with single-engined fighters. Once the Bf110 was adapted as a night fighter and equipped with an upward-firing cannon it achieved considerable success against RAF bombers. A total of 6,050 had been built by the closing stages of the war, when production stopped.

HEINKEL He111

The He111 was originally designed in response to demands at the time of the Luftwaffe's birth for a fast airliner capable of minimum adaptation to a bomber. The He111A medium-bomber version, which first flew in late 1935, possessed a performance better than many of the then current fighters. The early version He111-B1 had a stepped-up cockpit and flew in the Spanish Civil War.

The He111P had a completely redesigned nose which did away with the stepped windshield and introduced the fully-glazed offset nose bubble. By 1939, the He111H medium bomber version, fitted with two 1,350hp (1,006kW) Junkers Jumo 211F.2 inline piston engines, was being delivered. This was the most successful of the He111 range and on the outbreak of the Second World War it was well established with operational units. The bomb load was one 2,000kg (4,409lb) bomb carried externally and one 500kg (1,102lb) bomb carried internally, or eight 250kg (551lb) bombs all carried internally.

During the Battle of Britain the Luftwaffe had an average strength of some 500 He111s across seventeen Gruppen. It lost around 246 of its number in the course of the four-month battle. From mid September 1940, He111s had been largely confined to night bombing because of the high daytime losses and the Luftwaffe's 'beam-bombing' which gave increased accuracy. The He111 was a good medium bomber, but was kept in production long after it should have been replaced. Production ceased in 1944 after more than 7,300 had been built.

A pair of Heinkel He111Ps of III/KG255 with 25+B33 in the foreground.

23 SEPTEMBER

German fighter-bombers made sweeps against London, reportedly losing sixteen aircraft. With London under attack, the Cabinet ordered Bomber Command to drop parachute mines on Berlin.

By the beginning of the Battle of Britain the more powerful Heinkel He111H was quickly replacing the interim He111P.

DORNIER Do17

The Dornier Do17 was originally designed as a fast mail plane for Deutsche Lufthansa, which refused to accept it; so, the Do17 was quickly redesigned as a bomber. First flown in 1934, the initial production bomber model was the E-1, which was built in parallel with the F-1 reconnaissance version. In 1937, it was able to outpace contemporary fighters. Initially it had in-line engines, but in 1939 a return was made to BMW V1 7.3 12-cylinder liquid-cooled radial engines for the Do17Z and the export version, the Dornier Do215. At the outbreak of the Second World War, 370 Do17Z 'flying pencils' and undelivered Do215s equipped Luftwaffe operational units. Its advantages were speed and a sturdy construction; but by 1940 it was not fast enough to escape the RAF's fighters and was poorly armed, though it was shown that it could absorb much punishment.

Dornier Do17Zs were poorly armed and not fast enough to escape the RAF's fighters, but could absorb much punishment.

JUNKERS Ju87 STUKA

One of the best-known German aircraft of the Second World War, the single-engined Ju87 Stuka (Sturzkampfflugzeug, meaning dive bomber) featured a gull wing and fixed undercarriage. With a crew of two, it was designed to provide army support. The first Ju87 was flown in 1935, ironically powered by a British Rolls-Royce Kestrel engine. The Ju87B, with its 1,200hp Junkers Jumo 211Da 12-cylinder liquid-cooled engine, was the first quantity production version for the Luftwaffe and was prominent

24 & 26 SEPTEMBER

The Supermarine Woolston and Itchen works were bombed in daylight raids. Spitfire manufacture was then dispersed over a wide area of southern England, with production set up in garages and other small units requisitioned by the Ministry of Aircraft Production (MAP).

in the opening campaigns of the war. When operating under ideal conditions of air superiority, the Stuka was a formidable weapon with its big bomb load, but its success in Poland, France and the Low Countries blinded some of its advocates to its shortcomings. The aircraft, with its slow top speed and poor rate of climb, met its match when faced with the RAF's Spitfires and Hurricanes, and Ju87 units were decimated during the Battle of Britain. Despite its increasing obsolescence the aircraft continued to serve in other theatres. Over 5,700 Ju87s of all marks were produced and there can be no doubting its important contribution to the Luftwaffe's war effort.

30 SEPTEMBER

In addition to raids on London, Weybridge and Slough, a large attack was again launched against the Westland Aircraft factory at Yeovil. With cloud obscuring the target, the thirty He111s dropped their bombs on nearby Sherborne, Dorset. By the end of the day the last major daylight battle was over. Forty-seven Luftwaffe aircraft had been destroyed for the loss of twenty RAF fighters and eight pilots killed. By this date the Luftwaffe was down to 276 combat-ready fighters, while the RAF had 732.

Weather-beaten Ju87Bs of 8/Stuka 2 'Immelmann' returning from a raid.

A Ju87B-1 Stuka showing its distinctive dihedral wings, spatted fixed undercarriage and glasshouse cockpit.

JUNKERS Ju88

The Junkers Ju88 was one of the most versatile aircraft of the Second World War. It made its maiden flight on 31 December 1936 and entered service as a bomber and reconnaissance aircraft with the Luftwaffe in 1939. Its first action was on 26 September 1939, when a Ju88 attacked the British Fleet in the Firth of Forth; its bombs failed to detonate.

From small beginnings the Ju88 served in many roles including bomber, night fighter, reconnaissance, torpedo bomber, dive bomber, intruder, ground support and mine layer. Ju88s made several unescorted attacks against British airfields during the Battle of Britain. Although able to evade even a Spitfire by diving, the Ju88 suffered heavy losses at the hands of RAF fighters (albeit significantly lower than the attrition suffered by other German bombers committed to the Battle of Britain) and armour protection and defensive armament were subsequently increased. A total of 15,000 were built, of which over 9,000 were bomber variants – more than all other German bomber types combined – and the aircraft was still in production in 1945.

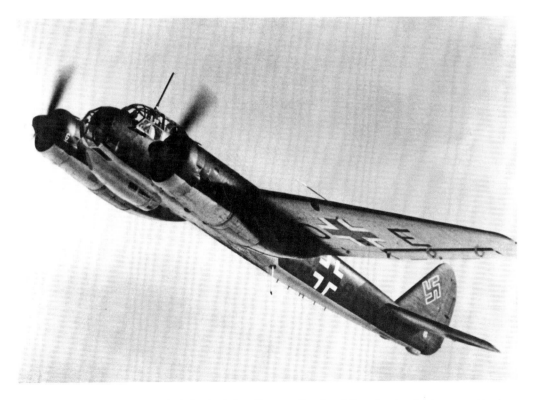

Over 15,000 Junkers Ju88s were built for the Luftwaffe, more than for all the other bomber types combined.

27 SEPTEMBER

Heavy attacks were made by eighty aircraft on Bristol and 300 on London. The Luftwaffe was reported to have lost fifty-five fighters and bombers.

13 THE BATTLE OF BRITAIN MEMORIAL FLIGHT

E stablished in 1957, the RAF Battle of Britain Memorial Flight pays enduring tribute to the many thousands of airmen who gave their lives in the service of their country. Its current fleet includes six Spitfires, two Hurricanes, a Douglas Dakota and Europe's only airworthy Avro Lancaster, which between them carry out hundreds of public engagements each year.

Based at RAF Woodvale, the Temperature and Humidity Flight, operated by a division of Short Bros, made its last monitoring flight in June 1957. The unit's Spitfire PRXIXs, PM631, PS853 and PS915, were flown by their civilian pilots to Duxford and ownership of them passed back to the RAF. The following month, escorted by Hunters and Javelins, the Spitfire trio arrived at RAF Biggin Hill and formed, with Hurricane IIc LF363, what was initially known as the Historic Aircraft Flight (HAF). Two months later, Spitfire PRXIX PS915 was removed for ground display purposes at RAF West Malling.

Three Spitfire XVIs (TE330, TE476 and SL574) that had been exhibited at the 1957 Royal Tournament, joined the flight and were brought back to flying condition at the instigation of RAF Biggin Hill's then station commander, Wing Commander Peter Thompson DFC. On 21 February 1958

1-31 OCTOBER

Every day of the month Fighter Command was involved in combat with Luftwaffe fighters and bombers, resulting in the loss of 186 RAF aircraft, while Germany lost nearly double that number.

Spitfire XIX PM631 and Hurricane IIc LF363 were the first of thier respective types to join the Historic Aircraft Flight.

One of three Spitfire XVIes that flew with the Battle of Britain Flight, TE476 was photographed at Coventry in July 1958.

the HAF was officially renamed the Battle of Britain Flight (BBF) just a week before RAF Biggin Hill closed as an active fighter base. As a result, on 28 February that year, the three Spitfire XVIs flew to RAF North Weald. The Hurricane and Spitfire PRXIX PM631 joined them on 3 March, having been delayed at Biggin Hill by a sudden fall of snow. The BBF then lost Mk XIX PS853 (flown to RAF West Raynham for gate guardian duties) and Mk XVI TE330 (withdrawn and sent to the USAF Academy). After barely two months at North Weald the flight moved again, this time to RAF Martlesham Heath, arriving on 16 May.

It was from Martlesham Heath that Spitfire XVI SL574, whilst leading the annual Battle of Britain flypast over London with Hurricane LF363 on 20 September 1959, suffered an engine failure that resulted in a forced landing on a cricket pitch in Bromley, Kent. This aircraft never flew again and both it and the other Mk XVI TE476, which had had a landing accident some ten days prior, were retired. There was yet another move on 3 November 1961, this time to RAF Horsham St Faith (which is today Norwich International Airport). With just a single Spitfire PRXIX (PM631) and Hurricane LF363 left, the flight's future looked bleak, but with its true value to the RAF reconsidered, steps were taken to revitalise the fleet. Horsham St Faith's closure on 1 April 1963 prompted relocation to RAF Coltishall. Here the Battle of Britain Flight began to prosper again, starting with Spitfire XIX PS853's return in April 1964 from West Raynham where it had been kept in flying condition. In that year the two Spitfires and Hurricane appeared at fifty displays around the country, a fraction of the commitments now undertaken by the much-expanded fleet.

The following year saw a third Spitfire added, this was the former Vickers Armstrong Ltd-owned Mk Vb AB910. It was flown to Coltishall by Jeffrey Quill, the test pilot who had been responsible for so much of the Spitfire's development flying. The making of the film *Battle of Britain* in 1968 was also a considerable boost for the BBF. All its aircraft were used at the various film locations, appearing with several different squadron codes. Additionally, the extensive search for well preserved airframes

Spitfire XIX PM631 taking part in the first Air Tattoo at North Weald in May 1971.

Spitfire XVIe SL574 after it made a forced landing on 20 September 1959.

3 OCTOBER

A lone Ju88 bombed the de Havilland factory at Hatfield, killing or injuring more than ninety workers and destroyed most of the materials for the new Mosquito.

Spitfire Vb AB910 photographed with the Flight at Exeter soon after it was given by Vickers, in June 1965.

Spitfire IIa P7350 at RAF Colerne's Battle of Britain 'At Home' Day display in September 1959.

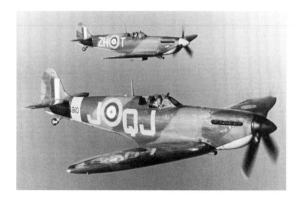

The BBMF's oldest Spitfires, Mk Vb AB910 in No. 92 Squadron markings and Mk IIa P7350 with No. 266 Squadron code letters. Both were flown in the film *Battle of Britain* in 1968.

Hawker gave Hurricane IIc PZ865 *The Last of the Many* to the Battle of Britain Flight in 1972.

With the addition of Lancaster PA474 in 1973, the Flight's name was changed to Battle of Britain Memorial Flight.

The BBMF had its first Spitfire IX, LF IXc MK356, airworthy in November 1997. It was then painted entirely silver.

7 OCTOBER

There was a large raid on the Westland Aircraft factory at Yeovil, during which seven enemy aircraft were shot down.

which preceded the filming revealed a Mk II Spitfire (P7350) in the museum at RAF Colerne. It was in such good condition that it was made airworthy for the film and afterwards it too joined the Flight, bringing the Spitfire strength to four. P7350 is the only one of the flight's aircraft that actually saw combat in the Battle of Britain, having served with No. 266 Squadron at Hornchurch in 1940.

Although the position of the Spitfire was now much healthier, the Hurricane's situation was less certain. In 1972 the Hawker Aircraft Company came to the rescue. It had retained the last Hurricane to come off the production line and used it in support of company projects until retiring it to its own museum in the late 1960s. Recognising the BBMF's plight, Hawkers completely refurbished this aircraft (PZ865, aptly named *The Last of the Many*) and presented it to the flight at Coltishall.

The next year, Lancaster B1 PA474 arrived at Coltishall. It had been returned to airworthiness by No. 44 Squadron – the RAF's first operational unit, which was equipped with Lancasters in 1942. With PA474 in place, the Battle of Britain Memorial Flight title was adopted and the format in which the flight still appears today was brought into being. One final move took the flight to RAF Coningsby – its permanent home from 1976 onwards. Spitfire XIX PS915 was 'rescued' in 1984 and restored by British Aerospace at Samlesbury, rejoining the Battle of Britain Memorial Flight in April 1987.

The first of two Chipmunk T10s, WK518, joined the flight in April 1983, with WG486 following twelve years later. With the Battle of Britain Memorial Flight's fighter pilots mainly having current fast-jet experience, the Chipmunks provide them with essential training in piston engine and tailwheel handling techniques. 1985 saw the addition of DH Devon C2 VP981 which until 1993 was used in support of long-distance displays not involving the Lancaster. The former Royal Aircraft Establishment Dakota III ZA947 was the next acquisition. It was obtained in July 1993 and began flying at air displays the following year.

In September 1991, Hurricane LF363 had an engine failure whilst flying from Coningsby to Jersey, crash-landed at RAF Wittering and was almost completely destroyed by the fire that ensued. It was rebuilt at Duxford over the next seven years, flying again on 29 September 1998. To help finance this restoration programme, Spitfire XIX PS853 was sold to a private owner and subsequently to Rolls-Royce, in whose charge it remains today. Two more Spitfires have since joined the flight – LF IXc MK356, a veteran of the June 1944 D-Day period in 1992, flying in November 1997, and LF XVIe TE311 in 2007, airborne after a long rebuild by the Battle of Britain Memorial Flight's engineers in 2012. The Battle of Britain Memorial Flight today operates five different types and twelve aircraft in total.

The most recent Spitfire to fly with the BBMF is LF XVIe TE311. It was painted in No. 74 Squadron colours coded 4D-V when first flown in October 2012.

8 OCTOBER

Sergeant Josef František, the highest scorer of enemy aircraft shot down in the Battle of Britain, was killed in a flying accident. A Czechoslovak Hurricane pilot with No. 303 (Polish) Squadron, he destroyed seventeen German aircraft.

14 OCTOBER
London's West End now shared its bombing experiences with the poorer sections of the capital. There were 900 fires in London that night.

BATTLE OF BRITAIN MEMORIAL FLIGHT AIRCRAFT

Spitfire IIa P7350

P7350 joined the Battle of Britain Memorial Flight in 1968, straight from the set of *Battle of Britain*. It wears the markings of No. 41 Squadron's Spitfire Ia N3162 with the code EB-G. Piloted by Flight Lieutenant Eric Lock, the original N3162 shot down three Luftwaffe aircraft during a single sortie on 5 September 1940.

Spitfire Vb AB910

AB910 was given to the Battle of Britain Memorial Flight in 1965. It is newly painted in the markings of No. 64 Squadron's Spitfire Vb BM327, coded SH-F. This was the personal aircraft of Flight Lieutenant Tony Cooper, who commanded A Flight in 1944.

Spitfire LFIXe MK356

MK356 joined the fleet in 1997. Its scheme is that of No. 126 Squadron's D-Day-striped Spitfire IXc ML214 *Kay*, coded 5J-K – that was Squadron Leader Johnny Plagis's personal aircraft.

Spitfire LFXVIe TE311

Having joined in 2007, TE311 was returned to flight in October 2012 and made its first public flying appearance the following year. It is painted to represent No. 74 Squadron's Spitfire XVIe TB675, coded 4D-V – the personal aircraft flown by No. 74 Squadron's commanding officer, Squadron Leader A.K. 'Tony' Reeves.

Spitfire PRXIX PM631

One of two 1957 Historic Aircraft Flight Spitfire PRXIXs still operated, PM631 appears in the markings of a No. 541 Squadron PRXIX tasked with photoreconnaissance sorties between early 1944 and September 1945.

Spitfire PRXIX PS915

The other remaining Spitfire PRXIX PS915, which first joined the flight in 1957, will fly in the colours of No. 81 (PR) Squadron's PS852 when it comes out of major overhaul in 2016. This is the aircraft in which Flight Lieutenant Ted Powles, AFC made sixty-three clandestine PR sorties over China in 1951 and achieved a world altitude record for piston engine aircraft (51,550ft) flying out of Kai Tak, Hong Kong, in February 1952.

Hurricane IIc LF363

The flight's first Hurricane, LF363 appears in the guise of No. 1 Squadron's Hurricane 1 P3395 with the code JX-B, as flown by Sergeant Pilot Arthur Clowes during the Battle of Britain.

Hurricane IIc PZ865

The last Hurricane built, PZ865 has been with the flight since 1972. It is painted to represent No. 34 Squadron South East Asia Command's Hurricane IIc HW840, coded EG-S. The original HW840's pilot was Flight Lieutenant Jimmy Whalen.

Hurricane IIc LF363 painted as a Hurricane I of No. 17 Squadron in the summer of 1940.

A different look to the Hurricanes LF363 and PZ865 at the 1983 International Air Tattoo at Greenham Common.

Lancaster B1 PA474

With the Lancaster's arrival in 1973, the flight adopted the name Battle of Britain Memorial Flight. PA474's present scheme is that of No. 617 Squadron's Lancaster DV385, coded KC-A and named *Thumper III.* It also carries the City of Lincoln coat of arms design, acknowledging that city's adoption of the Lancaster in 1975.

Dakota III ZA947

ZA947 joined the Battle of Britain Memorial Flight in July 1993 from the RAE and, repainted, made its air show debut the next year. It currently carries the D-Day invasion markings worn by No. 233 Squadron's Dakota FZ692 *Kwicherbichen* (*Quit Your Bitching*).

17 OCTOBER
Having been undecided about proceeding with the invasion (Operation *Sea Lion*), Hitler issued the order that 'from now until spring, preparations for *Sea Lion* shall be continued solely for the purpose of maintaining military and political pressure on Britain'.

Dakota ZA947 joined the BBMF in July 1993. It currently carries the D-Day invasion markings worn by No. 233 Squadron's Dakota FZ692 *Kwicherbichen*.

The BBMF's ever-popular opening flypast – the Lancaster accompanied by a Spitfire and Hurricane.

Chipmunk T10 WG486

WG486 became part of the BBMF in 1995, joining WK518 as one of the RAF's last two serving Chipmunks. Both examples provide BBMF Spitfire and Hurricane pilots with ongoing tailwheel-handling experience.

Chipmunk T10 WK518

WK518 came to the BBMF at RAF Coningsby in April 1983. Its current paint scheme recreates that worn during this aircraft's time with Hull University Air Squadron some fifty years ago.

31 OCTOBER

The Battle of Britain was officially over. Mainly due to the success of the RAF, the conditions necessary for Hitler's invasion had not been created. During the month the Luftwaffe lost 317 aircraft and Fighter Command 144. The tide had turned.